Place Value Through Hundred Thousands

You can write numbers in different ways.
312,501 can be written in:

Standard Form	Use digits—**312,501**
Word Form	Use words—**three hundred twelve thousand, five hundred one**
Short Word Form	Use digits and words—**312 thousand, 501**
Expanded Form	Use digits to show the value of each place **300,000 + 10,000 + 2,000 + 500 + 1 = (3 × 100,000) + (1 × 10,000) + (2 × 1,000) + (5 × 100) + (1 × 1)**

Write each number in standard form.

1. 415 thousand, 25

2. 800,000 + 4,000 + 60 + 2

3. 100,000 + 900 + 20 + 3

_____   _____   _____

4. three hundred forty-seven thousand, one hundred five _____

Write the value of the underlined digit in short word form.

5. 1<u>3</u>7,294

6. <u>5</u>63,089

7. 426,<u>7</u>18

_____   _____   _____

Write the number in word form, short word form, and in expanded form.

8. 702,946 _____

Problem Solving

9. At times, the earth is two hundred thirty-eight thousand, eight hundred fifty-seven miles from the moon. Write this number in standard form.

_____

Show Your Work

Use with text pages 4–5.

More About Place Value

> ### You can use exponents to write numbers.
>
> $10^4 = 10 \times 10 \times 10 \times 10 = 10{,}000$
>
> **You can use exponents to write 872,596 in expanded form.**
>
> $(8 \times 10^5) + (7 \times 10^4) + (2 \times 10^3) + (5 \times 10^2) + (9 \times 10^1) + (6 \times 10^0)$

Use exponents to write each number in expanded form.

1. 19,742 _____

2. 617,945 _____

3. 56,067 _____

Write each number in standard form.

4. $(4 \times 10^5) + (9 \times 10^4) + (5 \times 10^3) + (7 \times 10^2) + (6 \times 10^1) + (3 \times 10^0)$ _____

5. $(2 \times 10^4) + (1 \times 10^3) + (8 \times 10^2) + (5 \times 10^1) + (1 \times 10^0)$ _____

What is the value of n in each equation?

6. $60{,}000 = 6 \times 10^n$ _____

7. $5^2 \times 3 = n$ _____

Problem Solving

8. Are 10^0 and 2^0 equal? Why or why not?

Show Your Work

_____   _____

Use with text pages 6–7.

Place Value Through Hundred Billions

Different Ways to Write Numbers.

Standard Form	20,650,389,260
Word Form	twenty billion, six hundred fifty million, three hundred eighty-nine thousand, two hundred sixty
Short Word Form	20 billion, 650 million, 389 thousand, 260
Expanded Form	$(2 \times 10,000,000,000) + (6 \times 100,000,000) + (5 \times 10,000,000) +$ $(3 \times 100,000) + (8 \times 10,000) + (9 \times 1,000) + (2 \times 100) + (6 \times 10)$
Expanded Form with Exponents	$(2 \times 10^{10}) + (6 \times 10^8) + (5 \times 10^7) + (3 \times 10^5) +$ $(8 \times 10^4) + (9 \times 10^3) + (2 \times 10^2) + (6 \times 10^1)$

Write each number in standard form.

1. 42 billion, 126 million, 3 thousand, 13 _____

2. seven hundred fifteen billion, two hundred four million, one hundred two _____

3. $(6 \times 10^9) + (3 \times 10^7) + (1 \times 10^6) + (7 \times 10^4) + (2 \times 10^3) + (9 \times 10^1)$ _____

Write the value of the underlined digit in short word form.

4. 813,709,426 _____

5. 68,091,352,426 _____

Use exponents to write the number in expanded form.

6. 91,726,482 _____

Problem Solving

7. Canada has a land area of about nine million, nine hundred eighty-four thousand, six hundred seventy square kilometers. Write that number in standard form.

_____

Show Your Work

Use with text pages 8–9.

Compare, Order, and Round Whole Numbers

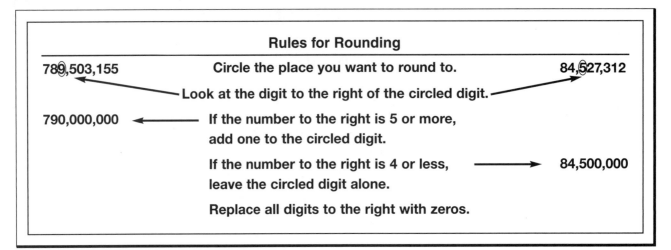

Rules for Rounding

| 789,503,155 | Circle the place you want to round to. | 84,527,312 |

Look at the digit to the right of the circled digit.

790,000,000 ◀──── If the number to the right is 5 or more, add one to the circled digit.

If the number to the right is 4 or less, ──▶ 84,500,000
leave the circled digit alone.

Replace all digits to the right with zeros.

Compare. Write >, <, or = for each ◯.

1. 24,981 ◯ 24,810

2. 734,556 ◯ 734,655

3. 45,813,540 ◯ 48,513,450

4. 2,198,070 ◯ 2,189,007

Order each set of numbers from greatest to least.

5. 9,254; 9,542; 9,515

6. 18,229; 18,209; 18,299

_____

_____

Round to the place indicated by the underlined digit.

7. 22,0_1_5,899 _____

8. 9_9_6,842,176 _____

Write a number for the missing digit that will make the inequality true.

9. 8_3,174 < 893,173

10. 265,_13 > 265,631

Problem Solving

Show Your Work

11. A toy company had a profit of $259,304 this year and $254,509 last year. Which profit was greater? Explain.

_____

Use with text pages 10–12.

Place Value Through Thousandths

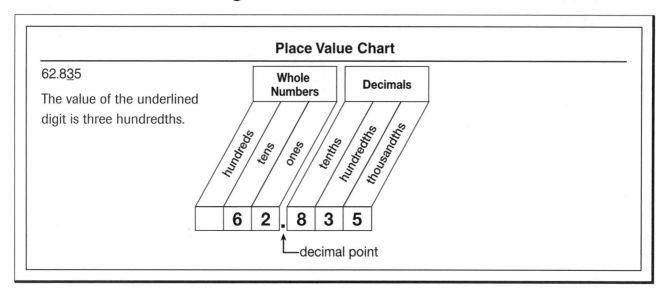

Place Value Chart

62.8**3**5

The value of the underlined digit is three hundredths.

Whole Numbers | Decimals

hundreds | tens | ones | tenths | hundredths | thousandths

6 | 2 . 8 | 3 | 5

└─decimal point

Write each in standard form.

1. twelve and fifty-four hundredths _____

2. six and sixteen thousandths _____

3. one hundred sixty-two thousandths _____

4. twenty and five hundredths _____

Write each decimal in words.

5. 23.6 _____

6. 8.002 _____

7. 10.01 _____

8. 2.112 _____

Write the value of the underlined digit in words.

9. 8.14_7_ _____

10. 515._4_2 _____

Problem Solving

Show Your Work

11. A laser measured Karen's height as forty-nine and seventeen thousandths inches. Write this height as a decimal.

_____

Use with text pages 14–15.

Problem-Solving Strategy:
Find a Pattern

To find a pattern in a word problem, ask yourself:	
Understand	What facts do I know?
	Can I find a pattern?
Plan	Did I describe the pattern?
Solve	Did I continue the pattern?
Look Back	Did I solve the problem?

Find a pattern to solve each problem.

Show Your Work

1. Mr. Santos is driving from Atlanta, Georgia to Phoenix, Arizona. On the first day, he drove 183 miles. He drove 213 miles on the second day, and 243 miles on the third day. If this pattern continues, how many miles will Mr. Santos drive on the fifth day?

   Explain your thinking. _____

   _____

   _____

2. Oakdale School is sponsoring a canned food drive. In the first week of the drive, the students collected 638 cans. They collected 698 cans in the second week and 758 cans in the third week. If the students continue to collect cans at this rate, in which week will they collect more than 1,000 cans?

   Explain your thinking. _____

   _____

   _____

Use with text pages 16–18.

Compare, Order, and Round Decimals

Compare Decimals

To compare 0.56 and 0.6:

Step 1   Align the decimal points.   0.56

                                              0.60

                                              ↑

Step 2   Start from the left.

                  Compare the digits until they are different.

Since $5 < 6$, $0.56 < 0.6$.

Compare. Write $>$, $<$, or $=$ for each $\bigcirc$.

1. 7.23 $\bigcirc$ 7.2   **2.** 0.145 $\bigcirc$ 0.45   **3.** 0.081 $\bigcirc$ 0.81

4. 0.9 $\bigcirc$ 0.900   **5.** 6.22 $\bigcirc$ 0.62   **6.** 5.073 $\bigcirc$ 5.307

Order the numbers from greatest to least.

7. 6.2; 6.02; 6 _____   **8.** 5.32; 0.325; 2.53 _____

9. 1.09; 11.9. 19.1 _____   **10.** 3.18; 0.83; 3.8 _____

Round to the place of the underlined digit.

11. 7.1<u>5</u>6 _____   **12.** 34.<u>2</u>77 _____   **13.** 0.<u>9</u>81 _____

Compare. Write $>$, $<$, or $=$ for each $\bigcirc$, given $a = 0.465$, $b = 0.8$, $c = 0.06$, and $d = 1$.

14. $a \bigcirc c$ **15.** $d \bigcirc b$ **16.** $a \bigcirc b$

Problem Solving

Show Your Work

17. Precious jewels are measured in carats. A jeweler has a ruby weighing 0.627 carats, a diamond weighing 0.82 carats, and a pearl weighing 0.092 carats. List the jewels in order from heaviest to lightest.

_____

Use with text pages 20–22.

Name _____ Date _____

Expressions and Addition Properties

You can write an algebraic expression for a word phrase.

Word Phrase   a number decreased by 5

Algebraic Expression   *n*   −   5

Write an algebraic expression for each word phrase.

1. add 12 to a number

2. 3 less than a number

3. 14 plus a number

4. 20 more than a number

5. take 16 from a number

6. a number reduced by 5

Translate each algebraic expression into words.

7. $k + 9$

8. $25 - a$

9. $x - 7$

10. $11 + b$

11. $h - 13$

12. $50 + c$

Evaluate each expression when $b = 18$. Then write $>$, $<$, or $=$ to compare the expressions.

13. $b - 0 \bigcirc 36 - b$

14. $24 - b \bigcirc b - 8$

15. $7 + b \bigcirc b + 7$

16. $(b + 5) + 4 \bigcirc b + (5 + 4)$

Problem Solving

Show Your Work

17. In Mrs. Campbell's class, there are 17 boys and some girls. Write an algebraic expression that describes the number of students in the class.

_____

Use with text pages 28–30.

Estimate Sums and Differences

Ways to Estimate a Sum or Difference		
Round to the greatest place.	**Round to a lesser place.**	**Use front-end estimation.**
3,278 rounds to 3,000	**3,278** rounds to 3,300	**3,278** rounds to 3,000
+1,634 rounds to +2,000	+**1,6**34 rounds to +1,600	+**1,6**34 rounds to +1,000
5,000	4,900	4,000

Estimate. Tell which method you used.

1.	746 +683	**2.**	957 −512	**3.**	8,315 +4,879	**4.**	6,114 −2,352

5.	4,085 +7,601	**6.**	7,020 −1,986	**7.** 57,308 − 29,554	**8.** $78 + $64

Estimate. Decide whether the sum is closer to 50 or 100.

9. 33 + 24   **10.** 54 + 46   **11.** 67 + 27   **12.** $41 + $13

_____   _____   _____   _____

Problem Solving

Show Your Work

13. A drama club sold 768 tickets to Friday's show and 922 tickets to Saturday's show. About how many tickets did the club sell altogether?

_____

Use with text pages 32–33.

Name _____ Date _____

Add and Subtract Whole Numbers

When adding or subtracting whole numbers, regroup when necessary.

$$\begin{array}{r} \overset{1\ 1\ 1}{5\,7,8\,4\,3} \\ +2\,4,1\,6\,5 \\ \hline 8\,2,0\,0\,8 \end{array}$$

$$\begin{array}{r} \overset{7\ 9\ 9\ 10}{1\,\cancel{8},\cancel{0}\,\cancel{0}\,\cancel{0}} \\ -1\,2,8\,4\,3 \\ \hline 5,1\,5\,7 \end{array}$$

Add or subtract. Check that your answer is reasonable.

1. 5,087
   +4,395

2. 8,914
   +6,382

3. 41,948
   + 8,655

4. 57,209
   +25,863

5. 868
   −599

6. 4,000
   −2,731

7. 84,306
   −55,704

8. 10,000
   − 3,629

9. 58,745 + 19,622

10. 30,134 − 24,868

_____

_____

Find each sum or difference when $n = 3,000,000$ and $s = 250$.

11. $n + 7$

12. $n + 7,000$

13. $n + 7,000,000$

_____

_____

_____

14. $1,000 − s$

15. $10,000 − s$

_____

_____

Problem Solving

Show Your Work

16. During the summer, the population of
    Spring Lake is 30,155. During the winter
    months, the population drops to 13,876.
    How many people spend only the
    summer months in Spring Lake?

_____

Use with text pages 34–36.

Name _____ Date _____

Add and Subtract Greater Numbers

When adding or subtracting greater numbers, choose either mental math, paper and pencil, estimation, a calculator, or a computer to solve the problem.

Estimate before you add or subtract. Round to the greatest place.

4,871,506 rounds to> 5,000,000   200,000 rounds to> 200,000
+1,349,005 rounds to> +1,000,000   − 65,815 rounds to> − 70,000
            Estimate   6,000,000   Estimate   130,000

Complete the addition and subtraction. Make sure to line up the ones digits.

4,871,506 + 1,349,005   200,000 − 65,815

```
  1 1 1    1
  4,8 7 1,5 0 6
+ 1,3 4 9,0 0 5
  6,2 2 0,5 1 1
```

```
  1 9 9  9 9 10
  2̷ 0̷ 0̷,0̷ 0̷ 0̷
−     6 5,8 1 5
    1 3 4,1 8 5
```

Add or subtract. Tell which method you used.

1.   708,214
   +290,528

2.   516,000
   − 25,772

3.   346,572
   +628,719

4.   6,050,100
   −1,342,800

5.   815,090
   +667,401

6.   275,000
   −125,000

7.   4,553,409
   +3,177,200

8.   6,927,000
   −2,000,000

9. 5,700,000 − 65,500

10. 360,000 + 640,000

Problem Solving

Use the table for Problem 11.

11. What is the estimated total population of the four towns listed to the right? Explain how you know.

Town	Population
Oakdale	87,430
Pleasantville	54,905
Springfield	42,887
Valley View	36,523

Use with text pages 38–39.

Name _____ Date _____

Addition and Subtraction Equations

You can make a model of the information. Use the model to write an equation.

Today, Aki read 6 more pages of her book than she read yesterday. Today she read 26 pages. How many pages did she read yesterday?

Today 26 pages	
Yesterday: n	Difference: 6

Yesterday + difference = today

$$n \quad + \quad 6 \quad = \quad 26$$
$$n \quad = \quad 20$$

Aki read 20 pages yesterday.

Write the equation shown by the model. Then solve the equation.

1.

28 children	
b	17 children

_____

2.

54	
29	k

_____

Use mental math to solve the equations. Use models if necessary.

3. $g + 7 = 32$ **4.** $84 - m = 52$ **5.** $21 + v = 41$ **6.** $r - 56 = 90$

_____   _____   _____   _____

7. $88 + j = 97$ **8.** $s - 47 = 83$ **9.** $\$2 + m = \$5$ **10.** $a - 100 = 0$

_____   _____   _____   _____

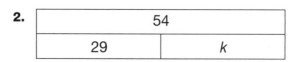

Problem Solving

Show Your Work

Write an equation to solve the problem.

11. Shannon had a coupon for popcorn at the movies. The original price of the popcorn was $3.10. Shannon only had to pay $1.75. What was the value of the coupon?

_____

Use with text pages 40–41.

Problem-Solving Decision:
Relevant Information

Ask Yourself

- What is the question?
- What do you need to know?
- What do you not need to know?

Draw a model to solve. If there is not enough information, tell what information is needed.

1. Mrs. Davis went to the show with $35. She bought a picture frame for $5 and a wreath for $12. She also bought lunch at the show. How much money did Mrs. Davis spend?

Show Your Work

_____

_____

_____

---

2. During the first two days of the show, 1,238 raffle tickets were sold. If 665 tickets were sold on the first day, how many tickets were sold on the second day?

_____

_____

_____

Use with text pages 42–43.

Expressions and Multiplication Properties

Properties of Multiplication		
Commutative Property	$a \times b = b \times a$	$6 \times 7 = 7 \times 6$
Associative Property	$a \times (b \times c) = (a \times b) \times c$	$2 \times (3 \times 5) = (2 \times 3) \times 5$
Identity Property	$a \times 1 = a$	$8 \times 1 = 8$
Zero Property	$a \times 0 = 0$	$4 \times 0 = 0$

Write an expression for each.

1. a number divided by 6

2. a number multiplied by 9

3. a number increased by 7

_____   _____   _____

4. twelve times a number

5. 55 more than a number

6. a number divided by 15

_____   _____   _____

Simplify. Tell which property you used.

7. $5 \times (20 \times 12)$

8. $35 \times 6 \times 0$

9. $25 \times 7 \times 4$

_____   _____   _____

10. $1 \times 19 \times 2$

11. $10 \times 13 \times 10$

12. $(9 \times 5) \times 2$

_____   _____   _____

Evaluate each expression, given $a = 6$, $b = 3$, and $c = 4$.

13. $a \times (b + c)$ _____

14. $(a \times b) + c$ _____

Problem Solving

Show Your Work

15. Alan and three friends split the cost of a
gift equally. Write an expression that
shows how much each person contributed
for the gift. Then use the expression to
determine how much Alan contributed if
the gift cost $48.

Use with text pages 80–80.

Name _____ Date _____

Model the Distributive Property

Distributive Property	
$a(b + c) = (a \times b) + (a \times c)$	$\begin{aligned} 8 \times 24 &= 8 \times (20 + 4) \\ &= (8 \times 20) + (8 \times 4) \\ &= 160 \quad + \quad 32 \\ &= 192 \end{aligned}$

Use the Distributive Property to multiply. Show the partial products for each and find the sum. Then write a multiplication sentence for each.

1.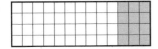

2.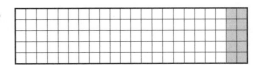

3.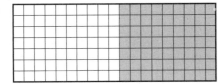

4.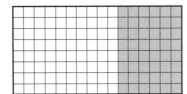

Draw and divide a rectangle to show each product. Use the Distributive Property to find the product.

5. 3×17

6. 6×24

Use with text pages 62–63.

Problem-Solving Strategy:
Use Logical Reasoning

	Ask Yourself
Understand	What facts do I know?
Plan	Will a table help me solve the problem?
Solve	What questions do I need to ask myself as I use the tables? Does my table include enough information?
Look Back	Does the solution make sense?

Use logical reasoning to solve each problem.

Show Your Work

1. Rico is a member of a soccer team, a chess club, a school band, and a drama club. Each group meets on a different weekday. Rico has no meetings on Friday. Drama meets the day before soccer. The band does not meet on Thursday. Chess does not meet on Tuesday or Wednesday. Soccer meets on Wednesday. What meeting does Rico have each weekday?

   Explain your thinking.

   _____

2. Bessie, Liang, Maria, and Seth have one backpack each. Each backpack is a different color. Maria's backpack is not black. Bessie's backpack is not green or blue. Liang's backpack is yellow. Seth's backpack is not green. What color is each person's backpack?

   Explain your thinking.

   _____

16 **Use with text pages 64–66.**

Multiply by One-Digit Numbers

Ways to Multiply by a One-Digit Number

$$\begin{array}{r} \overset{3\ 1}{3\,8\,4} \\ \times\qquad 4 \\ \hline 1,5\,3\,6 \end{array}$$

$$
\begin{aligned}
4 \times 384 &= 4 \times (300 + 80 + 4) \\
&= (4 \times 300) + (4 \times 80) + (4 \times 4) \\
&= \quad 1,200 \ + \ 320 \ + \ 16 \longleftarrow \text{partial product} \\
&= \quad 1,536
\end{aligned}
$$

Find the product.

1. $\begin{array}{r}95 \\ \times\ 7 \\ \hline\end{array}$	**2.** $\begin{array}{r}58 \\ \times\ 6 \\ \hline\end{array}$	**3.** $\begin{array}{r}561 \\ \times\ 9 \\ \hline\end{array}$	**4.** $\begin{array}{r}737 \\ \times\ 5 \\ \hline\end{array}$
5. $\begin{array}{r}3,815 \\ \times\quad 4 \\ \hline\end{array}$	**6.** $\begin{array}{r}7,462 \\ \times\quad 8 \\ \hline\end{array}$	**7.** $\begin{array}{r}16,529 \\ \times\qquad 3 \\ \hline\end{array}$	**8.** $\begin{array}{r}27,832 \\ \times\qquad 6 \\ \hline\end{array}$

9. $285,115 \times 3$

_____

10. $2 \times 474,691$

_____

Complete the function table.

11. Rule: $y = 3x$

x	218	785	3,946	6,148	12,552
y	_____	_____	_____	_____	_____

Use the Distributive Property to rewrite each expression. Then solve.

12. $7 \times 2,393$

13. $52,816 \times 4$

Problem Solving

Show Your Work

14. There are 144 notebooks in one carton.
How many notebooks are in 8 cartons?

_____

Use with text pages 68–70.

Patterns in Multiples of 10

Different Ways to Multiply Multiples by 10

Multiply. $7 \times 4{,}000 = n$

Use a pattern.	Use mental math.
$7 \times 4 = 28$	$7 \times 4{,}000 = 7 \times 4 \times 1{,}000$
$7 \times 40 = 280$	$= 28 \times 1{,}000$
$7 \times 400 = 2{,}800$	$= 28{,}000$
$7 \times 4{,}000 = 28{,}000$	

Use a pattern or mental math to find each product.

1. $\begin{array}{r} 70 \\ \times\ 8 \\ \hline \end{array}$

2. $\begin{array}{r} 600 \\ \times\ \ 9 \\ \hline \end{array}$

3. $\begin{array}{r} 5{,}000 \\ \times\ \ \ \ 6 \\ \hline \end{array}$

4. $\begin{array}{r} 9{,}000 \\ \times\ \ \ \ 5 \\ \hline \end{array}$

5. $\begin{array}{r} 30 \\ \times 80 \\ \hline \end{array}$

6. $\begin{array}{r} 500 \\ \times\ 70 \\ \hline \end{array}$

7. $\begin{array}{r} 900 \\ \times\ 90 \\ \hline \end{array}$

8. $\begin{array}{r} 6{,}000 \\ \times\ \ \ 80 \\ \hline \end{array}$

Multiply.

9. 37×60

10. 55×80

11. 728×30

12. 641×70

_____ _____ _____ _____

13. 398×20

14. 566×50

15. 813×40

16. 435×60

_____ _____ _____ _____

Problem Solving

17. Ed and his brother are participating in a bike-a-thon for charity. They will each bike 40 miles a day for 15 days. How far will they bike altogether?

Show Your Work

_____

Use with text pages 72–73.

Estimate Products

Different Ways to Estimate Products						
Front-end Estimation		**Rounding**		**Find a Range**		
84	80	84	80	84	80	90
×37	× 30	×37	× 40	×37	× 30	× 40
	2,400		**3,200**		**2,400**	**3,600**

Estimate by using front-end estimation. Then estimate by rounding.

1. 26 × 49   **2.** 53 × 45   **3.** 18 × 79   **4.** 32 × 21

_____   _____   _____   _____

5. 43 × 629   **6.** 85 × 442   **7.** 653 × 27   **8.** 831 × 56

_____   _____   _____   _____

Estimate. Give a range which includes the actual product. Then find the actual product.

9. 23 × 79   **10.** 46 × 33   **11.** 71 × 19   **12.** 55 × 42

_____   _____   _____   _____

Problem Solving

Show Your Work

13. Every workday, Mr. Perez drives
134 miles to work and back. About
how far does he drive in a month
with 19 workdays?

_____

               Use with text pages 74–75.

Multiply by Two-Digit Numbers

Different Ways to Multiply Two-Digit Numbers

$$\begin{array}{r} \overset{1}{\underset{}{1\,\overset{2}{}}}\\ 147 \\ \times\ 24 \\ \hline 588 \\ +\ 2940 \\ \hline 3{,}528 \end{array}$$

$$\begin{aligned} 147 \times 24 &= 147 \times (20 + 4) \\ &= (147 \times 20) + (147 \times 4) \\ &= \quad 2{,}940 \ + \ 588 \\ &= \ \mathbf{3{,}528} \end{aligned}$$

Find each product. Estimate or use a calculator to check.

1. $\begin{array}{r} 65 \\ \times 29 \\ \hline \end{array}$

2. $\begin{array}{r} 86 \\ \times 51 \\ \hline \end{array}$

3. $\begin{array}{r} 75 \\ \times 32 \\ \hline \end{array}$

4. $\begin{array}{r} 94 \\ \times 17 \\ \hline \end{array}$

5. $\begin{array}{r} 346 \\ \times\ 27 \\ \hline \end{array}$

6. $\begin{array}{r} 591 \\ \times\ 54 \\ \hline \end{array}$

7. $\begin{array}{r} 229 \\ \times\ 65 \\ \hline \end{array}$

8. $\begin{array}{r} 198 \\ \times\ 22 \\ \hline \end{array}$

Use the Distributive Property to rewrite each expression. Then solve.

9. 35×27

10. 61×19

11. 214×73

12. 725×48

Problem Solving

13. A principal ordered 25 computers for her school. Each computer costs $859. How much did the computers cost?

Show Your Work

Use with text pages 76–78.

Problem-Solving Decision:
Explain Your Solution

Ask Yourself

- Can I estimate the answer?

- Is a range of estimates sufficient?

- Do I need an exact answer?

Solve. Explain your answer.

Show Your Work

1. A school band is holding a concert to raise money for new uniforms. Band members sold 480 tickets to the concert. If the uniforms cost $3,400, will a ticket price of $7 be enough to cover the cost? Explain your thinking.

   _____

2. A principal ordered 6 buses for a fifth grade field trip. There are 265 students and teachers going on the trip. Each bus holds a maximum of 48 passengers. Did the principal order enough buses for the outing? Explain your thinking.

   _____

3. Al wants to buy a new video system that costs $299. He works 14 hours a week after school. If Al is paid $6 per hour, will he have enough money to buy the system after 4 weeks? Explain your thinking.

   _____

Use with text pages 80–81.

Name _____   Date _____

Estimate Quotients

Estimate with Compatible Numbers			
Estimate.			$\frac{300}{6\overline{)1,800}}$
$1,759 \div 6 = n$	Round the dividend to a multiple of 10 that can be divided easily by 6.	$1,800 \div 6 = n$	The estimated quotient is 300.

Estimate the quotient.

1. $7\overline{)487}$ **2.** $5\overline{)408}$ **3.** $6\overline{)2,371}$ **4.** $8\overline{)3,297}$

_____   _____   _____   _____

5. $4\overline{)33,203}$ **6.** $3\overline{)11,955}$ **7.** $9\overline{)803,486}$ **8.** $7\overline{)361,912}$

_____   _____   _____   _____

9. $649 \div 8$ **10.** $2,479 \div 5$ **11.** $43,054 \div 6$ **12.** $208,997 \div 3$

_____   _____   _____   _____

Problem Solving

Show Your Work

13. Seth estimated the quotient of $17,475 \div 6$ as 3,000. What numbers did Seth use for the dividend and divisor to get this quotient? Is Seth's estimate less than or greater than the actual quotient? Tell how you found your answer.

Use with text pages 86–87.

One-Digit Divisors

Quotients with Remainders

Divide. $315 \div 6 = n$

If the dividend and divisor
are not compatible numbers,
then the quotient will
include a **remainder**.

$$
\begin{array}{r}
52\ \textbf{R3} \\
6\overline{)315} \\
-30 \\
\hline
15 \\
-12 \\
\hline
3
\end{array}
$$

Check: $(52 \times 6) + 3$
$312 + 3$
315

Divide and check.

1. $4\overline{)138}$

2. $6\overline{)502}$

3. $2\overline{)9{,}257}$

4. $9\overline{)71{,}824}$

5. $3\overline{)12{,}662}$

6. $5\overline{)614{,}578}$

7. $429 \div 7$

8. $3{,}191 \div 6$

9. $15{,}915 \div 8$

_____   _____   _____

Equations

The division statement $17 \div 4 \longrightarrow 4$ R1 can be rewritten as $(4 \times 4) + 1 = 17$. Write and
solve a division statement for each equation.

10. $4a + r = 27$ **11.** $5b + r = 39$ **12.** $2b + r = 21$ **13.** $3a + r = 12$

_____   _____   _____   _____

Problem Solving

Show Your Work

14. Mr. Salvi bought 181 protractors to use
with his classes. If he has 5 classes
with 31 students in each, how many
protractors does he have for each class?
Explain your answer.

Use with text pages 88–89.

Problem-Solving Application:
Use Operations

	Ask Yourself
Understand	What is the question?
	What do I know?
Plan	Is the information correct?
	Do I have all the information I need?
Solve	Which operation(s) should I use?
	Did I use the operations in the correct order?
Look Back	Did I check my answer?

Use the table for Problems 1–3.

Show Your Work

1. Juan made 16 birdhouses and 12 mailboxes to sell at a fair. He packed them together in cartons of 6. He also made 25 picture frames and 21 signs. Juan packed these together in cartons of 8. How many cartons will he take to the fair?

Juan's Craft Corner Prices	
Birdhouse	$18
Mailbox	$32
Picture Frame	$12
Welcome Sign	$15

_____

2. The materials needed to make one picture frame cost Juan $4. How much money will Juan make if he sells all 25 of his picture frames at the fair?

_____

3. Juan sold half of his mailboxes at the fair. If it costs Juan $13 to make one mailbox, how much money did he make at the fair?

_____

Use with text pages 90–91.

Divisibility

Divisibility Rules

A number is **divisible** by another number when the quotient is a whole number and there is no remainder. Any **factor** of a given number divides into that number with no remainder.

Tell if each number is divisible by 2, 3, 4, 5, 6, 9, or 10.

1. 712

2. 810

3. 388

4. 621

5. 524

_____

_____

_____

_____

_____

6. 460

7. 1,912

8. 5,700

9. 3,126

10. 1,890

_____

_____

_____

_____

_____

Use the table for Problems 11–12.

11. Yuri and other members of his class gathered a total number of cans that is divisible by 4. What grade is Yuri in?

_____

12. The cans from each grade are packed individually in boxes of 9. Which two grades' cans will have boxes that are partially full?

_____

Canned Food Drive Totals	
Grade	Cans Collected
3	668
4	670
5	702
6	585

Problem Solving

13. Conor said that a number divisible by 3 and by 9 is also divisible by 6. Do you agree with Conor? Tell why or why not.

_____

_____

_____

Show Your Work

Use with text pages 92–94.

Zeros in the Quotient

Quotients with Zeros
Divide. $1{,}421 \div 7 = n$

Sometimes you cannot divide after bringing down a digit from the dividend. You must put a zero in the quotient before bringing down the next digit.

```
      203
  7)1,421
   -14
      021   Multiply. 3 × 7
    - 21   Subtract. 21 − 21
       0   There is no remainder.
```

Check:
```
   203
 ×   7
 1,421
```

Divide.

1. $8\overline{)816}$

2. $3\overline{)912}$

3. $5\overline{)547}$

4. $2\overline{)6{,}016}$

5. $9\overline{)3{,}655}$

6. $7\overline{)56{,}765}$

7. $6\overline{)24{,}425}$

8. $9\overline{)639{,}045}$

9. $284 \div 7$

10. $4{,}555 \div 9$

11. $40{,}723 \div 8$

12. $534{,}042 \div 6$

_____   _____   _____   _____

Problem Solving

Show Your Work

13. A school band raised $257 in a bake sale and $695 in a patron drive. The band will use this money to buy new hats for the band members. If each hat costs $9, how many hats can the band purchase?

_____

Use with text pages 96–97.

Problem-Solving Strategy:
Guess and Check

Ask Yourself

Understand	What is the question?
	What facts do I know?
Plan	Can I use Guess and Check to solve the problem?
	Did I make a reasonable first guess?
Solve	Did I check to see whether my guess is correct?
	Did I use the results from the first guess to make a better guess?
	Can I organize my guesses into a table?
Look Back	Is my answer reasonable?
	Did I solve the problem?

Use the Ask Yourself questions to help you solve each problem.

1. Rosa has 120 red, white, and blue beads. She has three times more red beads than white beads. She has twice as many blue beads as white beads. How many of each kind of bead does Rosa have? Organize your guesses into a table. Did this help you solve the problem? Explain.

Show Your Work

_____

2. Janell spent $40 for an outfit. She paid for the items using $10, $5, and $1 bills. If she gave the clerk 10 bills in all, how many of each bill did she use? Organize your guesses into a table. Did this help you solve the problem? Explain.

_____

Use with text pages 98–100.

Solve Equations

Solving Equations

Solve $5n = 40$	**Solve** $54 \div n = 9$	**Solve** $n \div 8 = 6$
Think: What number times 5 equals 40?	Think: 54 divided by what number equals 9?	Think: What number divided by 8 equals 6?
$5 \times 8 = 40$	$54 \div 6 = 9$	$48 \div 8 = 6$
$n = 8$	$n = 6$	$n = 48$

Solve each problem.

1. Sue worked for 6 hours. She earned $42. How much does Sue earn per hour?
$6n = 42$

_____

2. Betty will be able to give each of her seven friends four fruit snacks. How many fruit snacks does she have?
$n \div 7 = 4$

_____

Use mental math to solve the equations.

3. $32 \div r = 4$

_____

4. $5p = 20$

_____

5. $n \div 7 = 3$

_____

6. $9b = 63$

_____

7. $s \div 6 = 6$

_____

8. $24 \div m = 3$

_____

9. $6t = 18$

_____

10. $5c = 35$

_____

Replace *n* with 8. Is the equation true? Write *yes* or *no*.

11. $45 \div n = 5$

_____

12. $7n = 56$

_____

13. $n \div 1 = n$

_____

14. $n \times n = 16$

_____

Problem Solving

Show Your Work

15. Ali read *n* pages of her book each day. She finished the 48-page book in 6 days. How many pages did Ali read each day?

_____

Use with text pages 102–104.

Divide by Multiples of 10, 100, and 1,000

Look for Patterns When Dividing by Multiples of 10, 100, and 1,000

Find 36,000 ÷ 4	Find 335,000 ÷ 1,000	Estimate 18,000 ÷ 500
36 ÷ 4 = 9	335,000 ÷ 1 = 335,000	18,000 ÷ 500
360 ÷ 4 = 90	335,000 ÷ 10 = 33,500	15 ÷ 5 = 3
3,600 ÷ 4 = 900	335,000 ÷ 100 = 3,350	15,000 ÷ 500 = 30
36,000 ÷ 4 = 9,000	335,000 ÷ 1,000 = 335	20 ÷ 5 = 4
		20,000 ÷ 500 = 40

The quotient is between 30 and 40.

Divide. Use patterns, basic facts, or multiples of 10.

1. 810 ÷ 9

2. 480 ÷ 60

3. 6,300 ÷ 900

4. 4,500 ÷ 500

_____   _____   _____   _____

5. 56,000 ÷ 700

6. 40,000 ÷ 8,000

7. 210,000 ÷ 3,000

8. 540,000 ÷ 9,000

_____   _____   _____   _____

9. $800\overline{)24,000}$

10. $3,000\overline{)180,000}$

11. $600\overline{)300,000}$

12. $9,000\overline{)360,000}$

Use compatible numbers and multiples of 10 to estimate each quotient.

13. 34,600 ÷ 70

14. 431,000 ÷ 6,000

15. 789,000 ÷ 185

_____   _____   _____

Problem Solving

16. In Middletown, there is one principal for every 500 students. Middletown School District has 4,000 students. How many principals are there?

_____

Show Your Work

Use with text pages 110–111.

Two-Digit Divisors

Divide 768 ÷ 23.

$$
\begin{array}{r}
3 \\
23\overline{)768} \\
-69 \\
\hline
7
\end{array}
$$

$$
\begin{array}{r}
33\ \mathbf{R9} \\
23\overline{)768} \\
-69 \\
\hline
78 \\
-69 \\
\hline
9
\end{array}
$$

Check: $(33 \times 23) + 9 = 768$
$759 + 9 = 768$
$768 = 768$

Divide. Check your answer.

1. $24\overline{)85}$

2. $38\overline{)97}$

3. $29\overline{)62}$

4. $44\overline{)91}$

5. $13\overline{)528}$

6. $56\overline{)619}$

7. $64\overline{)947}$

8. $51\overline{)872}$

9. $238 \div 12$

10. $726 \div 36$

11. $493 \div 22$

12. $938 \div 29$

_____ _____ _____ _____

Problem Solving

13. Last year, Max spent $336 on video games. If each game cost $48, how many video games did Max buy last year?

Show Your Work

_____

Use with text pages 112–113.

Problem-Solving Strategy: Work Backward

	Ask Yourself
Understand	What is the question? What facts do I know?
Plan	Can I start with the facts I learned from the end of the problem and work backward? Can I use a model?
Solve	Did I start at the end of the problem with facts I know and work backward through the problem?
Look Back	Did I solve the problem?

Solve.

Show Your Work

1. Mr. Ruiz was principal of Wilson High for 6 years. He became principal after teaching at the school for 13 years. He first began teaching two years after graduating from college in 1973. During what years was Mr. Ruiz principal of Wilson High? Explain your thinking.

_____

2. At a concession stand, 37 more bottles of water were sold than cans of soda. There were 19 fewer cans of soda sold than cans of juice. There were 98 cans of juice sold. How many bottles of water were sold? Explain your thinking.

_____

3. Chloe's score on a math test was 5 points higher than Deb's score. Beth's score was 11 points lower than Chloe's score. Mandy's score was 3 points higher than Beth's score. Deb scored 92 on the test. What was each girl's test score? Explain your thinking.

_____

Use with text pages 114–116.

Adjusting Quotients

Estimate the quotient and adjust if necessary.

Quotient Too Large	Quotient Too Small

$$
\begin{array}{r} 3 \\ 26\overline{)710} \\ -78 \end{array}
\quad \rightarrow \quad 78 > 71 \quad \rightarrow \quad
\begin{array}{r} 2 \\ 26\overline{)710} \\ -52 \\ \hline 19 \end{array}
\qquad
\begin{array}{r} 4 \\ 17\overline{)895} \\ -68 \\ \hline 21 \end{array}
\quad \rightarrow \quad 21 > 17 \quad \rightarrow \quad
\begin{array}{r} 5 \\ 17\overline{)895} \\ -85 \\ \hline 4 \end{array}
$$

Divide. Check your answer.

1. $18\overline{)527}$ **2.** $31\overline{)618}$ **3.** $22\overline{)785}$ **4.** $16\overline{)971}$

_____   _____   _____   _____

5. $94\overline{)278}$ **6.** $51\overline{)355}$ **7.** $38\overline{)672}$ **8.** $45\overline{)877}$

_____   _____   _____   _____

9. $514 \div 17$ **10.** $262 \div 58$ **11.** $723 \div 75$ **12.** $348 \div 29$

_____   _____   _____   _____

Problem Solving

13. Mark volunteered at the public library this summer. He worked 35 days and during those days he checked in 1,960 books. If he checked in an equal number of books each day, how many did he check in on his first day of work?

Show Your Work

_____

Use with text pages 118–119.

Division with Greater Numbers

Find 15,286 ÷ 37.

$$
\begin{array}{r}
4 \\
37\overline{)15{,}286} \\
-14\,8 \\
\hline
4
\end{array}
\qquad
\begin{array}{r}
41 \\
37\overline{)15{,}286} \\
-14\,8 \\
\hline
48 \\
-37 \\
\hline
11
\end{array}
\qquad
\begin{array}{r}
413\ \textbf{R5} \\
37\overline{)15{,}286} \\
-14\,8 \\
\hline
48 \\
-37 \\
\hline
116 \\
-111 \\
\hline
5
\end{array}
$$

Check: (413 × 37) + 5 = 15,286
  15,281 + 5 = 15,286
    15,286 = 15,286

Divide. Check your answer.

1. 56$\overline{)2{,}765}$

2. 23$\overline{)9{,}823}$

3. 16$\overline{)91{,}265}$

4. 42$\overline{)35{,}874}$

5. 30$\overline{)23{,}498}$

6. 142$\overline{)59{,}336}$

7. 5,682 ÷ 39

8. 6,058 ÷ 24

9. 45,720 ÷ 34

_____   _____   _____

Problem Solving

10. A local farm has 57 rows of soybean plants. If there are a total of 14,250 soybean plants, how many are in each row?

Show Your Work

_____

Use with text pages 120–122.

Order of Operations

Order of Operations

1. Simplify the terms within **parentheses.**	$(8 + 5) \times 2^3 - 3$
2. Simplify the terms with **exponents.**	$13 \times 2^3 - 3$
3. **Multiply** and **divide** from left to right.	$13 \times 8 - 3$
4. **Add** and **subtract** from left to right.	$104 - 3 = 101$

Remember: Please excuse my dear Aunt Sally (PEMDAS).

Simplify.

1. $(85 - 22) + 4^2$

2. $7 + (42 \div 6) \times 5$

3. $(55 - 14) + (18 \div 9)^2$

_____ _____ _____

4. $(51 \div 3) + (21 \div 7)$

5. $1,535 - (34 - 18) \times 4$

6. $92 - (58 - 14) + 13$

_____ _____ _____

7. $12^2 - (8 \times 7) + 5$

8. $(121 \div 11) + 5^2$

9. $257 + (3^2 \times 5) - 18$

_____ _____ _____

Write $>$, $<$, **or** $=$ **for each** $\bigcirc$.

10. $43 + (17 - 6) \bigcirc (43 + 17) - 6$ **11.** $(94 - 36) + 41 \bigcirc 94 - (36 + 41)$

12. $(5 \times 2^2) + 12 \bigcirc 5 \times (2^2 + 12)$ **13.** $(81 \div 9) \times 3 \bigcirc (81 \div 3) \times 1$

Evaluate the expressions given $x = 3$ **and** $y = 5$.

14. $4(x + y) - y^2 =$ _____   **15.** $(x^2 + y^2) - 20 =$ _____

16. $(2x + 3y) - y =$ _____

Problem Solving

17. When Anna simplified the expression
$7 \times 9 - 6 \times 4$, she said the result is 228.
Do you agree with Anna? Explain.

Show Your Work

Use with text pages 124–126.

Problem-Solving Application:
Interpret Remainders

When you solve a problem with a remainder, you need to decide how to interpret the remainder.

Ask Yourself

Understand   What is the question?
                 What facts do I know?

Plan   What operation will I use?
           How will I interpret the remainder?

Solve   Should the remainder be in the answer or should it be dropped?

Look Back   Did I interpret the remainder correctly so that the answer makes sense?

Solve. Explain how you decided to interpret each remainder.

Show Your Work

1. There are 295 students and teachers going on a field trip. Each bus holds 48 people. How many buses are needed for the trip?

   _____

2. Guides can take groups of up to 40 people on a nature hike. How many full groups were among the 295 students and teachers?

   _____

3. During the trip, the students and teachers drank 894 juice packs. The packs came in cartons of 24. How many cartons were opened during the trip?

   _____

Use with text pages 128–130.

Measurement Concepts

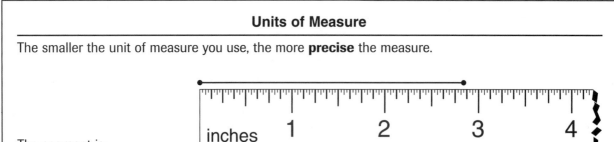

Units of Measure

The smaller the unit of measure you use, the more **precise** the measure.

The segment is:

- 3 inches long when measured to the nearest inch.
- $2\frac{3}{4}$ inches long when measured to the nearest quarter inch.

Decide what unit of measure to use. Then measure each item.

1. the width of this paper   _____

2. the length of your ring finger   _____

3. the width of the classroom door   _____

4. the length of a key   _____

5. the length of your leg from heel to knee _____

Tell whether a more precise measurement is needed or if an estimate is sufficient. Explain your answer.

6. You need to find the width of a piano to see   _____
if it will fit through a doorway.

7. You need to know the distance from your   _____
house to school to see about how far you travel
each day.

Problem Solving

Show Your Work

8. If you were having your feet measured   _____
for shoes, would you need to have a
more precise measure? Would a quarter
inch short make a big difference?
Explain.

Use with text pages 148–149.

Customary Units of Length

	How many feet are in 288 inches?	How many feet are in 4 yards 2 feet?
12 inches (in.) = 1 foot (ft)		
3 feet = 1 yard (yd)	Remember: Divide to change from a smaller to a larger unit.	Remember: Multiply to change from a larger to a smaller unit.
5,280 feet = 1 mile (mi)	288 in. = ☐ ft	4 yd 2 ft = ☐ ft
1,760 yards = 1 mile	288 ÷ 12 = 24	4 × 3 = 12
	288 in. = 24 ft	12 ft + 2 ft = 14 ft

Complete.

1. _____ ft = 6 yd

2. 3 mi = _____ ft

3. 24 yd = _____ ft

4. 114 in. = _____ ft _____ in.

5. 8,000 ft = _____ mi _____ ft

6. 180 in. = _____ ft

Compare. Write >, <, or = for each ○.

7. 6 ft ○ 72 in.

8. 150 in. ○ 15 ft

9. 2 mi ○ 10,000 ft

Which unit would you use to measure each? Write *inch*, *foot*, *yard*, or *mile*.

10. the length of a puppy _____

11. the length of a soccer field _____

12. the width of your state _____

13. the height of a van _____

Problem Solving

Show Your Work

14. Gayle has 5 yd 2 ft of wire. Mae has 204 in. of wire. Who has more wire? Explain how you found your answer.

Use with text pages 150–151.

Customary Units of Weight and Capacity

Customary Units of Weight	Customary Units of Capacity
16 ounces (oz) = 1 pound (lb)	8 fluid ounces (fl oz) = 1 cup (c)
2,000 pounds = 1 ton (T)	2 cups = 1 pint (pt)
	2 pints = 1 quart (qt)
	4 quarts = 1 gallon (gal)

Complete.

1. 15 pt = ___ qt ___ pt   **2.** 30 qt = ___ gal ___ qt   **3.** 14 c = ___ pt

4. 72 oz = ___ lb ___ oz   **5.** 13,200 T = ___ T ___ lb **6.** ___ pt = 12 qt

Compare. Write >, <, or = for each ◯.

7. 100 oz ◯ 6 lb   **8.** 5 T ◯ 10,000 lb   **9.** 9 c ◯ 5 pt

Which unit would you use to measure each? Write *oz, lb, T, fl oz, c, pt, qt,* or *gal.*

10. Capacity of a bathtub _____   **11.** Weight of a truck _____

12. Your weight _____   **13.** Capacity of a juice box _____

Problem Solving

Show Your Work

14. Jake needs 25 cups of apple juice for a class party. How many quarts of juice should he buy?

_____

Use with text pages 152–154.

Metric Units of Length

Metric Units of Length	Changing Metric Units of Length	
10 millimeters (mm) = 1 centimeter (cm)	Multiply to change from a larger to a smaller unit.	Divide to change from a smaller to a larger unit.
10 centimeters = 1 decimeter (dm)	4 km = ☐ m	500 mm = ☐ cm
10 decimeters = 1 meter (m)	4 × 1,000 = 4,000	500 ÷ 10 = 50
1,000 meters = 1 kilometer (km)	4 km = 4,000 m	500 mm = 50 cm

Use a ruler. Measure each line segment to the nearest decimeter, centimeter, and millimeter.

1. •————————————————————————————————•

_____

2. •————————————————————————————————•

_____

3. •————————————————————————•

_____

4. •————————————————————————————•

_____

Complete.

5. 55 m = ____ dm   6. ____ cm = 20 mm   7. 9 m = ____ cm

Compare. Write >, <, or = for each ◯.

8. 50 cm ◯ 5 dm   9. 8 km ◯ 9,000 m   10. 200 dm ◯ 2 m

Problem Solving

Show Your Work

11. Name a distance you would measure in kilometers and a distance you would measure in meters.

Use with text pages 156–159.

Metric Units of Mass and Capacity

Metric Units of Mass	Metric Units of Capacity
1,000 milligrams (mg) = 1 gram (g)	1,000 milliliters (mL) = 1 liter (L)
1,000 grams = 1 kilogram (kg)	10 deciliters (dL) = 1 liter (L)
1,000 kilograms = 1 metric ton (t)	

Complete.

1. 8 L = ____ dL

2. ____ t = 6,000 kg

3. 9 g = ____ mg

4. ____ L = 50,000 mL

5. 8 kg = ____ g

6. 20 t = ____ kg

Compare. Write >, <, or = for each ○.

7. 16 dL ○ 160 L

8. 7 kg ○ 700 g

9. 13 t ○ 13,000 kg

Tell which metric unit you would choose to measure each. Explain your choice.

10. amount of juice in a large pitcher _____

11. mass of a car _____

12. mass of a box of cereal _____

13. amount of honey on a spoon _____

Problem Solving

Show Your Work

14. The mass of Box A is 3 kg. The mass of Box B is 2 kg 550 g. The mass of Box C is 3,500 g. How would you list the boxes from least to greatest mass? Tell how you found your answer.

Use with text pages 160–162.

Add and Subtract Measurements

Ask Yourself

• Are the units the same? $2\ g - 400\ mg = 2{,}000\ mg - 400\ mg = 1{,}600\ mg$

• Do I need to regroup or simplify?   8 ft 3 in. + 2 ft 10 in. = 10 ft 13 in. = 11 ft 1 in.

Add or subtract.

1.   6 L 8 dL
    + 9 L 7 dL

2.   8 yd 1 ft
    − 3 yd 2 ft

3.   5 T 1,800 lb
    + 1 T   550 lb

4.   7 h 15 min
    − 2 h 40 min

5.   3 g 800 mg
    + 9 g 700 mg

6.   14 m 1 dm
    − 8 m 9 dm

7. 2 gal − 3 pt

8. 4 yd − 2 ft 3 in.

9. 9 lb 10 oz + 2 lb 12 oz.

_____   _____   _____

Find the length represented by z.

10. $6\ yd - z = 2\ yd\ 2\ ft$

11. $z - 2\ km = 1\ km\ 700\ m$

12. $3\ ft - z = 9\ in.$

_____   _____   _____

Problem Solving

Show Your Work

13. Mina poured 8 fl oz of juice concentrate into a 2-quart pitcher. How much water should she add to fill the pitcher? Tell how you found your answer.

       Use with text pages 164–165.

Problem-Solving Decision:
Multistep Problems

Ask Yourself		
Understand	What is the question?	
	What data do I need to use to solve the problem?	
Plan	Which operation or operations do I need to use to solve the problem?	
Solve	Did I do the operations in the correct order?	
Look Back	Did I answer the question?	
	Does my answer make sense?	

Use the schedule to solve. Show all your steps.

Station	Bus 115	Bus 228	Bus 317
Mount Holly	7:15 A.M.	8:38 A.M.	7:45 A.M.
Springfield	7:28 A.M.	— — — —	7:58 A.M.
Millerville	— — — —	9:02 A.M.	8:25 A.M.
Oceanside	8:37 A.M.	9:42 A.M.	9:05 A.M.

Show Your Work

1. Tom and Leon both travel from
   Springfield to Oceanside. Tom takes Bus
   115 while Leon takes Bus 317. Whose
   trip takes more time? How much more?

   _____

   _____

2. Deb, Sarah, and Jane all live in Mount
   Holly and work in Oceanside. Deb takes
   Bus 228, Sarah takes Bus 317, and Jane
   takes Bus 115. How would you list the
   females from shortest to longest trip?

   _____

   _____

Use with text pages 166–167.

Double Bar Graphs

Steps to Making a Double Bar Graph

Step 1: Draw the axes.

Step 2: Choose an appropriate scale and mark equal intervals.

Step 3: Label the horizontal axis with the information the bars show.

Step 4: Draw the bars.

Step 5: Make a key to help observers read the graph. Give the graph a title.

Use the graph for Problems 1–7.

1. How many students have Golden Retrievers?

   _____

2. What is the difference in the number of fifth- and sixth-graders who own Siberian Huskies?

   _____

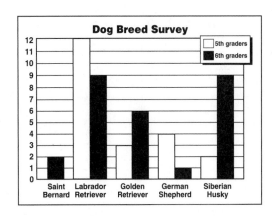

3. How many fifth-grade students own either a Labrador Retriever or a German Shepherd?

   _____

4. What two breeds are owned by a total of 16 fifth-grade students?

   _____

5. What breed has a total equal to the number of sixth-grade students who own a Siberian Husky?

   _____

6. Why was only one bar drawn above the label *Saint Bernard?*

   _____

Problem Solving

7. How many students participated in the survey? Explain how you found your answer.

Show Your Work

Use with text pages 172–175.

Histograms

Steps to Making a Histogram

Step 1: Draw the axes. Label the vertical axis. Choose an appropriate scale and mark equal intervals.

Step 2: Label the horizontal axis and list the intervals.

Step 3: Draw a bar for each interval. Do not leave spaces between the bars.

Step 4: Give the graph a title.

Use the graph for Problems 1–8.

1. How many students exercise between 6 and 10 times a month?

   _____

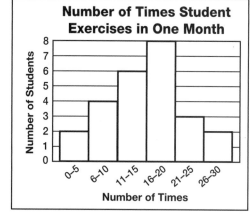

2. How many more students exercise between 16 and 20 times a month than between 26 and 30 times a month?

   _____

3. How many students exercise 10 or fewer times a month?

   _____

4. How many students exercise more than 20 times a month?

   _____

5. What three intervals have a total equal to the number of students who exercise between 16 and 20 times a month?

   _____

6. How many students were surveyed?

   _____

7. How would you list the intervals from least to greatest number of students?

   _____

Problem Solving

Show Your Work

8. Why does the histogram end with a maximum of 30 times a month?

   _____

Use with text pages 176–177.

Line and Double Line Graphs

Steps to Making a Line Graph

Step 1: Draw the axes. Label the horizontal axis and the vertical axis. Choose an appropriate scale and mark equal intervals.

Step 2: Draw the points. Connect the points with a straight line.

Step 3: Give the graph a title.

Use the graph for Problems 1–6.

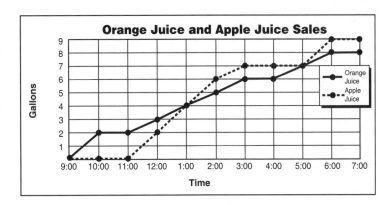

1. How many gallons of apple juice were sold at 12:00?

   _____

2. At what times were orange juice and apple juice sales equal?

   _____

3. Between 9:00 and 11:00, how many more gallons of orange juice were sold than apple juice?

   _____

4. How many gallons of apple juice were sold between 1:00 and 4:00?

   _____

5. What pattern occurs in the amount of apple juice sold between 11:00 and 2:00?

   _____

Problem Solving

6. How many gallons of juice were sold between 9:00 and 7:00? Tell how you found your answer.

   _____

Show Your Work

Use with text pages 178–180.

Choose an Appropriate Graph

Different Types of Graphs

A **bar graph** is appropriate when the data can be counted and you want to make comparisons.

A **line graph** is appropriate when you want to show change over time.

A **pictograph** is a good choice when the data are multiples of a number.

A **circle graph** is a good choice when the data are parts of a whole.

A **histogram** is a good choice to show how frequently data occur within equal intervals.

Choose an appropriate graph for the data.

1.

Event	Mass
Javelin	0.8 kg
Discus	2.0 kg
Shot Put	7.26 kg
Hammer	7.26 kg

_____

2.

Time	Number of Students
10–12 sec	3
13–15 sec	5
16–18 sec	10
19–21 sec	6
22–24 sec	2

_____

3.

Event	Record
Javelin, women's	74.68 m
Javelin, men's	89.66 m
Discus, women's	72.30 m
Discus, men's	68.82 m
Shotput, women's	22.41 m
Shotput, men's	22.47 m

_____

4.

Sport	Number of Students
Baseball	16
Football	8
Soccer	12
Softball	4
Hockey	4
Total	44

_____

Problem Solving

5. If you wanted to make a pictograph for the data set in Problem 4, how many students should each picture represent? Explain why.

_____

Show Your Work

Use with text pages 182–183.

Misleading Graphs

Misleading Graphs

A **misleading graph** shows data in a false, or misleading, way.

To see if a graph is misleading, ask yourself:

• Does the graph have a zigzag line to show that numbers are missing from the scale?

• Does the graph have a scale with equal intervals?

---

1. The two graphs show the same information. Which graph seems misleading? Explain.

_____

Use the smaller graph for Problems 2–3.

2. Tell why it seems that more than four times more visitors came to the Science Fair on Sunday than on thursday.

_____

3. How many more visitors went to the fair on Saturday than on Thursday? How many more went on Sunday than on Friday? Do the bars accurately show these differences? Tell why or why not.

_____

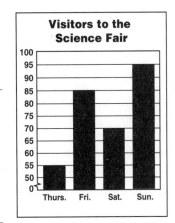

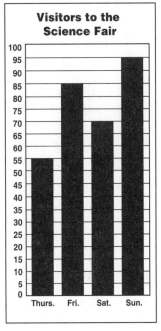

Problem Solving

Show Your Work

4. Change the intervals of the misleading graph above from 5 to 50. Would this affect the appearance of the graph? Is the graph still misleading? Explain your answer.

_____

Use with text pages 184–185.

Problem-Solving Decision:
Relevant Information

Use the relevant information in the bar graph to the right to solve. Show your work.

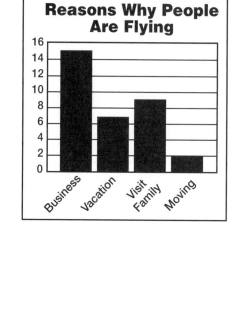

Reasons Why People Are Flying

1. The number of people who fly to visit family is equal to the number of people who fly for what two reasons?

   _____

   _____

2. How would you list the reasons why people fly from least to greatest?

   _____

   _____

   _____

3. How many people participated in the survey? Tell how you found your answer.

   _____

   _____

48   **Use with text pages 186–187.**

Collect and Organize Data

Steps to Making a Survey

Step 1: Decide on a survey question.

Step 2: List five or six answer choices for the question on a recording sheet.

Step 3: Pose the survey question to group of people. Use a tally mark to record each answer.

Step 4: Count the tally marks for each answer. Record the total in the Frequency column.

Step 5: Analyze the results.

The table shows the results of a survey of a fifth-grade class. Use the table for Problems 1–6.

1. Complete the Frequency column of the table.

2. How many of those surveyed have read exactly two books?

   _____

3. Which answer choices received an equal number of votes? How many votes did each receive?

   _____

Number of Books Read	Tally	Frequency
1					
2							
3									
4						
5				
More than 5	|||	

4. How many people responded to the survey?

   _____

5. How many more people gave the most popular answer choice than the least popular answer choice?

   _____

Problem Solving

6. Would the results of this survey be different if the question were asked of children between the ages of 3 and 5? Tell why or why not.

   _____

   _____

Show Your Work

Use with text pages 192–193.

Mean, Median, Mode, and Range

Mean	Sum of the numbers divided by the number of addends	**Make a Line Plot to Organize Data**
Median	Middle number when data is arranged in order	**Step 1:** List the data in order.
Mode	Number that occurs most often	**Step 2:** Make a number line that covers the range of numbers in your list.
Range	Difference between the greatest and least values	**Step 3:** Put an X above each number as many times as that number appears in the list.
Cluster	Several data points in a small interval	
Gap	A large space between data	

Make a line plot on a separate sheet of paper for each set of data. Identify clusters and gaps. Then find the mean, median, mode, and range.

1. time in seconds

65, 57, 63, 60, 63, 65, 59, 61, 65

Mean _____

Median _____

Mode _____

Range _____

2. ages in years

4, 14, 29, 24, 20, 42, 21, 30, 14

Mean _____

Median _____

Mode _____

Range _____

Find the mean, median, and mode for each set of data.

3. 25, 83, 30, 84, 42, 87, 73, 69, 83

Mean _____

Median _____

Mode _____

4. 106, 98, 114, 111, 105, 98, 110

Mean _____

Median _____

Mode _____

5. 77, 75, 71, 82, 85, 89, 80, 72, 71

Mean _____

Median _____

Mode _____

Problem Solving

Show Your Work

6. Dixie claims to be able to determine the mode of data by simply looking at a line plot. Do you think this is possible? Tell why or why not?

_____

Use with text pages 194–196.

Make and Use a Stem-and-Leaf Plot

Steps to Making a Stem-and-Leaf Plot

Step 1: Write a title.

Step 2: Write the tens digits needed to represent the data in order from least to greatest. Each of these numbers is a **stem.**

Step 3: For each piece of data, write the ones digit, or **leaf,** next to its tens digit. Arrange the digits from least to greatest. Write a key.

7|4 means 74.

Number of Amusement Parks in Different Countries

Stem	Leaf
0	2 2 3 4 4 4 5 6 7
1	1 1 1 3 4 5 8
2	
3	8
4	7
5	
6	
7	4

Use the stem-and-leaf plot for Problems 1–5.

1. What does 1| 2 mean?

   _____

Number of Birds Observed by Each Group

Stem	Leaf
0	2 4
1	2 5 6 9
2	2 3 5 7 9 9 9
3	1 3

0|2 means 2.

2. How many groups observed fewer than 20 birds?

   _____

3. How many groups are represented in the data?

   _____

4. How many groups observed 25 or more birds?

   _____

5. What are the mean, median, mode, and range of these data?

   _____

Problem Solving

6. On the back of this paper, make a stem-and-leaf plot for this set of data: 12, 38, 26, 8, 9, 14, 27, 26, 11, 4, 24, 36. Explain how you can use your completed stem-and-leaf plot to find the mode of the data.

   _____

Show Your Work

Use with text pages 198–199.

Name _____   Date _____

Problem Solving Strategy:
Make a Table

Ask Yourself

Understand What facts do I know?

Plan Did I make a table with the correct headings and ranges?

Solve Did I tally the table?
Did I find the frequency for each range?

Look Back Did I check my answer?

Make a table to solve each problem.

1. Marcus asked his classmates how
   many hours they spend doing
   homework each week. His set
   of data is shown below.
   5, 6, 8, 10, 7, 6, 8, 2, 7, 11, 9, 6,
   3, 5, 14, 8, 9, 10, 4, 5, 7, 8, 12, 10

   Do most of his classmates spend from
   1 to 5 hours, from 6 to 10 hours,
   or from 11 to 15 hours on homework
   each week?

   _____

Make your table here.

卌 |

卌 卌 卌

|||

2. Dave recorded the ages of the first
   twenty people to enter a movie theater.
   His set of data is shown below.
   32, 18, 21, 25, 28, 15, 47, 55, 51, 29
   17, 19, 26, 22, 38, 61, 57, 35, 44, 33

   Were the ages of most of the people from
   1 to 10, 11 to 20, 21 to 30, 31 to 40,
   41 to 50, 51 to 60, or 61 and higher?

   _____

||||

卌 |

||||

||

|||

|

52

Name _____ Date _____

Draw Conclusions and Make Predictions

Ask Yourself

• Do most of the data center around one number or a few numbers?

• Which statistic best describes the typical number in the data—the mean, the median, or the mode?

Use the data from the line plot for Problems 1–3.

1. How many holes were played?

   _____

2. Find the mean, median, and mode of the data.

   Mean _____

   Median _____

   Mode _____

3. Use the mean, median, or mode to predict how many strokes you would need to complete a golf hole. Explain your answer. _____

_____

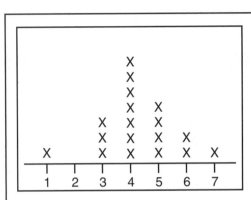

Number of Strokes to Complete One Golf Hole

Use the data from the table for Problems 4–7.

4. Show the data on a line plot.

Runs Scored by Tigers Baseball Team
9 6 2 8 7 3 5 1 4 6 2 6 5 7 4

5. What is the mean and median of the data?

   Mean _____

   Median _____

6. What is the mode and range of the data?

   Mode _____

   Range _____

Problem Solving

7. Suppose you were the coach of the next team the Tigers face. How many runs do you think your team needs to score in order to beat the Tigers? Give reasons for your answer.

   _____

Show Your Work

Use with text pages 204–206.

Prime and Composite Numbers

Find the factors of 50

- $50 \div 1 = 50$
- $50 \div 2 = 25$
- $50 \div 5 = 10$

Begin by trying to divide 50 by each number starting with 1.
Stop when a factor is repeated.

The factors of 50 are 1, 2, 5, 10, 25, and 50.
It is a composite number.

Write all the factors of each number. Then identify the number as *prime* or *composite*.

1. 9

_____

2. 16

_____

3. 20

_____

4. 29

_____

5. 33

_____

6. 37

_____

7. 42

_____

8. 45

_____

9. 49

_____

10. 51

_____

11. 68

_____

12. 99

_____

Problem Solving

Show Your Work

13. Scott has 72 baseball cards. He wants to display them in rows with an equal number of cards. How many different ways can Scott set up the rows?

_____

Use with text pages 224–225.

Prime Factorization

Write the prime factorization of 24.		
Step 1: Write 24 as the product of 2 factors.	**Step 2:** Write the factors of each composite factor.	**Step 3:** Write the prime factors. $24 = 2 \times 2 \times 2 \times 3$ $24 = 2^3 \times 3$

Complete the factor tree. Then write the prime factorization.

1.

```
    20
   /  \
  2 × ☐
 / \
2 × 2 × ☐
```
$2^☐ \times ☐$

2.

```
      20
     /  \
    4 × ☐
   / \
  ☐ × 2 × ☐
```
$☐^2 \times ☐$

Write the prime factorization of each number. Use exponents if possible. If the number is prime, write *prime.*

3. 28

_____

4. 23

_____

5. 30

_____

6. 42

_____

7. 65

_____

8. 56

_____

9. 100

_____

10. 81

_____

11. 41

_____

Problem Solving

12. Name two numbers whose prime factorization includes the numbers 2, 3, and 5. Write the prime factorization of each.

_____

Show Your Work

Use with text pages 226–227.

Greatest Common Factor

Different Ways to Find the GCF of 15 and 20		
Way 1: Make a list.		**Way 2:** Use prime factorization.
15: 1, 3, **5**, 15	The GCF is 5.	$15 = 3 \times 5$
20: 1, 2, 4, **5**, 10, 20		$20 = 2^2 \times 5$

List the factors of each number. Then find the greatest common factor of the numbers.

1. 16 _____

42 _____

_____

2. 21 _____

25 _____

_____

3. 24 _____ ,

56 _____

_____

4. 12 _____

30 _____

_____

Write the prime factorization using exponents of each number. Then find the greatest common factor (GCF) of the numbers.

5. 24 _____

36 _____

_____

6. 21 _____

56 _____

_____

7. 45 _____

81 _____

_____

8. 50 _____

75 _____

_____

Problem Solving

Show Your Work

9. Tia made 50 cupcakes and 160 cookies for a bake sale. She put the items in packages with an equal number of cupcakes and cookies. How many packages did she make? What was in each package?

_____

Use with text pages 228–230.

Least Common Multiple

Different Ways to Find the LCM of 8 and 20		
Way 1: Make a list.		**Way 2:** Use prime factorization.
8: 8, 16, 24, 32, **40**, 48	The LCM is 40.	$8 = \mathbf{2^3}$
20: 20, **40**, 60, 80, 100		$20 = 2^2 \times \mathbf{5}$
		$40 = 2^3 \times 5$

Write the first five multiples of each number.

1. 9

2. 13

3. 15

_____

_____

4. 21

5. 19

6. 50

_____

_____

Write the prime factorization of each number.

7. 14

8. 18

9. 48

_____

Find the LCM of the numbers in each pair. Use either method.

10. 15, 18

11. 12, 32

12. 15, 45

_____

13. 24, 40

14. 36, 72

15. 28, 42

_____

Problem Solving

16. Stacey jogs every third day and swims every fourth day. If she is jogging and swimming on Monday, what day of the week will she next end up jogging and swimming?

Show Your Work

_____

Use with text pages 232–234.

Fractions and Mixed Numbers

Improper Fractions and Mixed Numbers	
Divide to change an improper fraction to a mixed number.	Multiply and add to change a mixed number to an improper fraction.
$$4\overline{)9} \\ \underline{-8} \\ 1$$ So $\frac{9}{4} = 2\frac{1}{4}$	$2\frac{1}{4} = \frac{(4 \times 2) + 1}{4} = \frac{9}{4}$ So $2\frac{1}{4} = \frac{9}{4}$.

Study this number line. Write each missing fraction.

1.
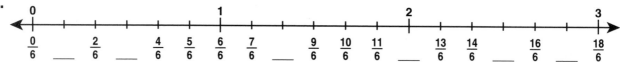

Write each improper fraction as a mixed number or a whole number.

2. $\frac{15}{4}$ _____

3. $\frac{19}{5}$ _____

4. $\frac{21}{7}$ _____

5. $\frac{20}{9}$ _____

6. $\frac{11}{3}$ _____

7. $\frac{26}{2}$ _____

8. $\frac{31}{5}$ _____

9. $\frac{21}{8}$ _____

Write each mixed number as an improper fraction.

10. $1\frac{4}{5}$ _____

11. $3\frac{1}{3}$ _____

12. $5\frac{5}{6}$ _____

13. $2\frac{7}{8}$ _____

14. $4\frac{1}{2}$ _____

15. $7\frac{3}{4}$ _____

16. $1\frac{9}{10}$ _____

17. $2\frac{7}{9}$ _____

Problem Solving

Show Your Work

18. A whole pizza has 8 slices. Tina has $3\frac{5}{8}$ pizzas. How many slices does she have?

_____

Use with text pages 236–238.

Name _____ Date _____

Equivalent Fractions and Simplest Form

To find equivalent fractions		
Multiply the numerator and denominator by the same number.	Divide the numerator and denominator by a common factor. 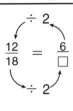 $$\frac{12}{18} = \frac{6}{9}$$	**Simplest form:** Divide numerator and denominator by greatest common factor (GCF). 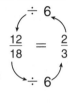

Complete.

1. $\frac{5}{8} = \frac{10}{\square}$

_____

2. $\frac{12}{15} = \frac{\square}{5}$

_____

3. $\frac{9}{18} = \frac{1}{\square}$

_____

4. $\frac{2}{3} = \frac{\square}{9}$

_____

5. $\frac{7}{10} = \frac{\square}{100}$

_____

6. $\frac{21}{27} = \frac{7}{\square}$

_____

7. $\frac{6}{30} = \frac{3}{\square}$

_____

8. $\frac{10}{25} = \frac{\square}{50}$

_____

Simplify each fraction.

9. $\frac{22}{4}$

_____

10. $\frac{20}{16}$

_____

11. $\frac{22}{32}$

_____

12. $\frac{45}{36}$

_____

13. $\frac{35}{15}$

_____

14. $\frac{42}{48}$

_____

15. $\frac{30}{9}$

_____

16. $\frac{40}{16}$

_____

Problem Solving

Show Your Work

17. Aidan had 40 out of 50 questions correct on a test. Write the number correct as a fraction in simplest form.

_____

Use with text pages 240–241.

Problem-Solving Strategy:
Use Logical Reasoning

Ask Yourself

Understand What facts do I know?

Plan How can I organize what I know so that I can use logical thinking?

Solve Can I draw a Venn diagram?
Did I label the parts of my diagram?
Did I find the factors of the two numbers?

Look Back Does my answer meet all the given conditions?
How can I check my answer?

Use logical thinking to solve each problem.

Show Your Work

1. Joe and Anna collect football cards.
   The GCF of the numbers of cards in their
   collections is 15. Altogether Joe and Anna
   have 75 cards. If Joe has more cards than
   Anna, how many cards do they each have?

   _____

2. The LCM of two numbers is 100. The
   GCF of the numbers is 1. The sum of the
   numbers is 29. What are the numbers?

   _____

3. Fraction $\frac{r}{s} = \frac{5}{8}$. $r + s = 39$. What are r and s?

   _____

Use with text pages 242–245.

Relate Fractions, Mixed Numbers, and Decimals

Decimals and Fractions	
Write a decimal as a fraction.	Write a fraction as a decimal.
$0.7 = \dfrac{7}{10}$ $0.55 = \dfrac{55}{100} = \dfrac{11}{20}$	$\dfrac{3}{4} = \dfrac{75}{100} = 0.75$ $\dfrac{9}{10} = 0.9$

Write each decimal as a fraction or mixed number in simplest form.

1. 0.42

2. 7.5

3. 0.38

4. 0.01

_____

_____

_____

_____

5. 6.18

6. 2.2

7. 0.6

8. 1.01

_____

_____

_____

_____

Write each fraction or mixed number as a decimal.

9. $\dfrac{9}{10}$

10. $5\dfrac{7}{50}$

11. $2\dfrac{4}{5}$

12. $6\dfrac{1}{4}$

_____

_____

_____

_____

13. $\dfrac{4}{25}$

14. $\dfrac{19}{50}$

15. $3\dfrac{11}{20}$

16. $\dfrac{13}{25}$

_____

_____

_____

_____

Problem Solving

Show Your Work

17. Write a decimal and a fraction to show what part of a dollar one penny represents. Write your answer in simplest form.

_____

Use with text pages 246–247.

Compare and Order Fractions and Decimals

Different Ways to Compare 2.4, $2\frac{1}{4}$, and 2.04

Way 1: Write the mixed number as a decimal.

$2\frac{1}{4} = 2.25$

Compare the decimals.

$2.04 < 2.25 < 2.4$

Way 2: Write the decimals as mixed numbers.

$2.4 = 2\frac{4}{10}$ $\qquad\qquad$ $2.04 = 2\frac{4}{100}$

Rename with a common denominator.

$2\frac{4}{10} = 2\frac{40}{100}$ $\qquad$ $2\frac{1}{4} = 2\frac{25}{100}$

Compare the mixed numbers.

$2\frac{4}{100} < 2\frac{25}{100} < 2\frac{40}{100}$

Compare. Write >, <, or = for each ◯.

1. $0.6 \bigcirc \frac{1}{5}$

2. $9.08 \bigcirc 9\frac{1}{5}$

3. $\frac{4}{5} \bigcirc 0.9$

4. $1\frac{7}{10} \bigcirc 1.07$

_____ _____ _____ _____

5. $2.5 \bigcirc 2\frac{1}{2}$

6. $1\frac{13}{20} \bigcirc 1.8$

7. $3.6 \bigcirc 3\frac{6}{100}$

8. $\frac{9}{25} \bigcirc 0.4$

_____ _____ _____ _____

Order each set of numbers from least to greatest.

9. $\frac{1}{2}, \frac{6}{10}, 0.2, 0.4$

10. $\frac{3}{10}, 0.75, 1.2, 1\frac{1}{10}$

_____ _____

11. $3.6, 3.55, 1.8, \frac{2}{10}$

12. $2.09, 2\frac{4}{5}, 2.5, 2\frac{9}{10}$

_____ _____

Problem Solving

13. On Monday, $\frac{4}{10}$ of the students bought lunch in the cafeteria. On Tuesday, 0.3 of the students bought lunch and on Wednesday, $\frac{3}{5}$ bought lunch. How would you list the days from least to most lunches purchased from the cafeteria?

Show Your Work

_____

Use with text pages 248–250.

Estimate With Fractions

Estimate $\frac{4}{5} + \frac{1}{8} + \frac{11}{20}$.	Estimate $65\frac{3}{4} - 23\frac{1}{2}$.
Round the fractions to 0, $\frac{1}{2}$, or 1.	Use front-end estimation.
$\frac{4}{5}$ is close to 1.	$\begin{array}{rr} 65\frac{3}{4} & 60 \\ -\ 23\frac{1}{2} & -20 \\ \hline & 40 \end{array}$
$\frac{1}{8}$ is close to 0.	
$\frac{11}{20}$ is close to $\frac{1}{2}$.	
$1 + 0 + \frac{1}{2} = 1\frac{1}{2}$	

Estimate the sum or difference. Name the method you used to estimate.

1. $\frac{13}{15} - \frac{3}{5}$

2. $6\frac{1}{2} + 8\frac{2}{3}$

3. $\frac{9}{10} + \frac{7}{8}$

_____ _____ _____

4. $45\frac{2}{3} - 34\frac{2}{7}$

5. $85\frac{5}{9} + 21\frac{1}{4}$

6. $\frac{6}{7} + \frac{2}{3} + \frac{1}{8}$

_____ _____ _____

7. $13\frac{4}{5} + 74\frac{2}{3}$

8. $\frac{4}{9} + \frac{8}{15} + \frac{9}{10}$

9. $59\frac{3}{4} - 18\frac{5}{6}$

_____ _____ _____

10. $\frac{6}{7} + \frac{2}{5} + \frac{5}{9} + \frac{1}{6}$

11. $84\frac{1}{5} + 37\frac{2}{3}$

12. $\frac{9}{20} + \frac{13}{15} + \frac{2}{11} + \frac{7}{8}$

_____ _____ _____

Problem Solving

Show Your Work

13. Meg made a quilt that is $50\frac{3}{4}$ inches long. She put $1\frac{7}{8}$ inches of trim along the edges of her quilt. About how long is it now?

_____

Use with text pages 256–257.

Add With Like Denominators

Add $3\frac{6}{7} + 1\frac{5}{7}$.

Step 1: Add the fractions.	**Step 2:** Add the whole numbers.	**Step 3:** Simplify.
$\begin{array}{r} 3\frac{6}{7} \\ + 1\frac{5}{7} \\ \hline \frac{11}{7} \end{array}$	$\begin{array}{r} 3\frac{6}{7} \\ + 1\frac{5}{7} \\ \hline 4\frac{11}{7} \end{array}$	$\begin{array}{r} 3\frac{6}{7} \\ + 1\frac{5}{7} \\ \hline 4\frac{11}{7} = 5\frac{4}{7} \end{array}$

Add. Write each sum in the simplest form.

1. $4\frac{3}{9} + 1\frac{5}{9}$

2. $5\frac{2}{8} + 2\frac{7}{8}$

3. $\frac{5}{12} + \frac{11}{12}$

_____

_____

_____

4. $\frac{2}{3} + 1\frac{1}{3}$

5. $\frac{8}{11} + \frac{7}{11}$

6. $6\frac{1}{5} + 3\frac{4}{5}$

_____

_____

_____

7. $\begin{array}{r} 3\frac{7}{10} \\ + 4\frac{9}{10} \\ \hline \end{array}$

8. $\begin{array}{r} \frac{7}{9} \\ + \frac{7}{9} \\ \hline \end{array}$

9. $\begin{array}{r} 5\frac{2}{3} \\ + 4\frac{2}{3} \\ \hline \end{array}$

10. $\begin{array}{r} 6\frac{5}{10} \\ + 3\frac{3}{10} \\ \hline \end{array}$

11. $\begin{array}{r} 7\frac{3}{4} \\ + 6\frac{1}{4} \\ \hline \end{array}$

12. $\begin{array}{r} 11\frac{9}{15} \\ + 7\frac{3}{15} \\ \hline \end{array}$

Problem Solving

13. Tani jogged $1\frac{3}{4}$ km on Tuesday and $2\frac{3}{4}$ km on Thursday. How far did he jog altogether?

Show Your Work

_____

Use with text pages 258–259.

Add Fractions With Unlike Denominators

Add $\frac{4}{5} + \frac{2}{3}$.

Step 1: Use the LCD to find equivalent fractions.

$$\frac{4}{5} = \frac{12}{15}$$
$$+ \frac{2}{3} = \frac{10}{15}$$

Step 2: Add the fractions.

$$\frac{12}{15}$$
$$+ \frac{10}{15}$$
$$\overline{\frac{22}{15}}$$

Step 3: Simplify.

$$\frac{22}{15} = 1\frac{7}{15}$$

Add. Write each sum in simplest form.

1. $\frac{2}{3} + \frac{2}{8}$

_____

2. $\frac{3}{4} + \frac{5}{8}$

_____

3. $\frac{9}{10} + \frac{3}{5}$

_____

4. $\frac{6}{10} + \frac{1}{2}$

_____

5. $\frac{5}{6} + \frac{7}{9}$

_____

6. $\frac{1}{3} + \frac{4}{10}$

_____

7. $\begin{array}{r} \frac{3}{10} \\ + \frac{9}{20} \\ \hline \end{array}$

8. $\begin{array}{r} \frac{6}{10} \\ + \frac{1}{4} \\ \hline \end{array}$

9. $\begin{array}{r} \frac{5}{8} \\ + \frac{5}{6} \\ \hline \end{array}$

10. $\begin{array}{r} \frac{2}{8} \\ + \frac{3}{4} \\ \hline \end{array}$

11. $\begin{array}{r} \frac{3}{5} \\ + \frac{1}{3} \\ \hline \end{array}$

12. $\begin{array}{r} \frac{9}{10} \\ + \frac{3}{15} \\ \hline \end{array}$

Problem Solving

13. A chef used $\frac{3}{4}$ cup of water and $\frac{1}{2}$ cup of milk in a recipe. How many cups of water and milk did she use altogether?

_____

Show Your Work

Use with text pages 260–261.

Add Mixed Numbers With Unlike Denominators

Add $2\frac{1}{6} + 3\frac{2}{3} + 1\frac{1}{4}$.

Step 1: Use the LCD to find equivalent fractions.

$$2\frac{1}{6} = 2\frac{2}{12}$$
$$3\frac{2}{3} = 3\frac{8}{12}$$
$$+ 1\frac{1}{4} = 1\frac{3}{12}$$

Step 2: Add the fractions.

$$2\frac{2}{12}$$
$$3\frac{8}{12}$$
$$+1\frac{3}{12}$$
$$\overline{\quad \frac{13}{12}}$$

Step 3: Add the whole numbers. Simplify.

$$2\frac{2}{12}$$
$$3\frac{8}{12}$$
$$+ 1\frac{3}{13}$$
$$\overline{6\frac{13}{12} = 7\frac{1}{12}}$$

Add. Write each sum in simplest form.

1. $3\frac{2}{3} + 1\frac{1}{4}$

2. $4\frac{1}{2} + 2\frac{3}{8}$

3. $7\frac{1}{3} + 3\frac{1}{2}$

_____ _____ _____

4. $1\frac{4}{5} + 2\frac{1}{2}$

5. $6\frac{3}{5} + 4\frac{7}{10}$

6. $5\frac{2}{3} + 1\frac{3}{4}$

_____ _____ _____

7. $\quad 9\frac{1}{2}$
$+ 4\frac{2}{3}$

8. $\quad 5\frac{3}{8}$
$+ 1\frac{3}{4}$

9. $\quad 1\frac{9}{10}$
$+ 7\frac{4}{5}$

10. $\quad 4\frac{3}{6}$
$\quad 2\frac{1}{3}$
$+ 1\frac{3}{4}$

11. $\quad 2\frac{3}{9}$
$\quad 4\frac{1}{2}$
$+ 5\frac{2}{3}$

12. $\quad 8\frac{5}{8}$
$\quad 7\frac{4}{5}$
$+ 1\frac{3}{10}$

Problem Solving

Show Your Work

13. Paulina used $4\frac{1}{2}$ yards of red cloth, $1\frac{3}{8}$ yards of white cloth, and $2\frac{3}{4}$ yards of blue cloth to make a costume. How much cloth did she use altogether?

_____

Use with text pages 262–264.

Subtract With Like Denominators

Find $7 - 3\frac{4}{5}$.

Step 1: Rename the whole number.

$$7 = 6\frac{5}{5}$$
$$- 3\frac{4}{5} = - 3\frac{4}{5}$$

Step 2: Subtract the fractions.

$$6\frac{5}{5}$$
$$- 3\frac{4}{5}$$
$$\frac{1}{5}$$

Step 3: Subtract the whole numbers. Simplify.

$$6\frac{5}{5}$$
$$- 3\frac{4}{5}$$
$$3\frac{1}{5}$$

Subtract. Write each difference in simplest form.

1. $8\frac{1}{16} - 3\frac{7}{16}$

_____

2. $9 - 3\frac{1}{4}$

_____

3. $7\frac{3}{5} - 2\frac{4}{5}$

_____

4. $6 - 1\frac{2}{3}$

_____

5. $8\frac{3}{7} - 6\frac{3}{7}$

_____

6. $5 - 4\frac{1}{9}$

_____

7.
$$\frac{9}{10}$$
$$- \frac{4}{10}$$

8.
$$\frac{7}{8}$$
$$- \frac{3}{8}$$

9.
$$8\frac{4}{5}$$
$$- 2\frac{1}{5}$$

10.
$$10$$
$$- 4\frac{2}{3}$$

11.
$$3\frac{1}{2}$$
$$- 1\frac{1}{2}$$

12.
$$7\frac{5}{9}$$
$$- 5\frac{2}{9}$$

Problem Solving

13. Russell has 5 m of wire. He used $3\frac{3}{4}$ m for a project. How much wire is left?

_____

Show Your Work

Use with text pages 266–267.

Subtract With Unlike Denominators

Find $\frac{4}{5} - \frac{3}{10}$.

Step 1: Use the LCD to find equivalent fractions.

$$\frac{4}{5} = \frac{8}{10}$$
$$-\frac{3}{10} = -\frac{3}{10}$$

Step 2: Subtract.

$$\frac{8}{10}$$
$$-\frac{3}{10}$$
$$\overline{\frac{5}{10}}$$

Step 3: Simplify.

$$\frac{8}{10}$$
$$-\frac{3}{10}$$
$$\overline{\frac{5}{10}} = \frac{1}{2}$$

Subtract. Write the difference in simplest form.

1. $\frac{3}{4} - \frac{1}{3}$

_____

2. $\frac{5}{8} - \frac{1}{4}$

_____

3. $\frac{2}{3} - \frac{1}{5}$

_____

4. $\frac{5}{12} - \frac{1}{6}$

_____

5. $\frac{8}{15} - \frac{1}{5}$

_____

6. $\frac{9}{10} - \frac{1}{4}$

_____

7. $\frac{17}{20}$
$-\frac{3}{5}$

8. $\frac{5}{6}$
$-\frac{2}{3}$

9. $\frac{7}{9}$
$-\frac{1}{3}$

10. $\frac{12}{15}$
$-\frac{1}{5}$

11. $\frac{3}{4}$
$-\frac{1}{6}$

12. $\frac{7}{10}$
$-\frac{1}{4}$

Problem Solving

13. Bella bought $\frac{3}{4}$ pound of nuts. Her family ate $\frac{1}{8}$ pound of the nuts. How much is left?

_____

Show Your Work

Use with text pages 268–269.

Problem-Solving Strategy: Draw a Diagram

	Ask Yourself
Understand	What facts do I know?
Plan	Did I draw a diagram?
Solve	How can I use my diagram to solve the problem?
Look Back	Did I solve the problem?
	Is my answer reasonable?

Draw a diagram to solve each problem.

Show Your Work

1. The Hawks soccer team practiced three times this week. On Tuesday, the team practiced for $\frac{3}{4}$ hour. On Thursday, the team practiced for $\frac{1}{2}$ hour more than it did on Tuesday. On Saturday, the team practiced twice as long as it did on both Tuesday and Thursday combined. Altogether, how long did the Hawks practice this week?

   _____

2. The Hawks have 18 players. Boys make up $\frac{5}{6}$ of the team. How many girls are on the Hawks?

   _____

3. The first week of practice, the team practiced 4 times. On Monday, they practiced for $\frac{1}{2}$ hour. On Wednesday, they practiced $1\frac{1}{2}$ times as long as they did on Monday. On Thursday and Friday combined, they practiced 3 times as long as they did on Monday. Altogether, how long did the Hawks practice the first week?

   _____

Use with text pages 270–272.

Subtract Mixed Numbers With Unlike Denominators

Find $5\frac{1}{2} - 1\frac{7}{8}$.

Step 1: Use the LCD to find equivalent fractions.

$$5\frac{1}{2} = \quad 5\frac{4}{8}$$
$$-1\frac{7}{8} = -1\frac{7}{8}$$

Step 2: Rename the mixed numbers.

$$5\frac{4}{8} = \quad 4\frac{12}{8}$$
$$-1\frac{7}{8} = -1\frac{7}{8}$$

Step 3: Subtract and simplify.

$$4\frac{12}{8}$$
$$-1\frac{7}{8}$$
$$\overline{3\frac{5}{8}}$$

Subtract. Write each difference in simplest form.

1. $\quad 9\frac{1}{2}$
   $\quad -3\frac{3}{8}$

2. $\quad 7\frac{1}{8}$
   $\quad -2\frac{3}{6}$

3. $\quad 7\frac{1}{5}$
   $\quad -2\frac{1}{8}$

4. $\quad 4\frac{1}{4}$
   $\quad -2\frac{5}{6}$

5. $\quad 9\frac{1}{8}$
   $\quad -2\frac{1}{3}$

6. $\quad 5\frac{4}{5}$
   $\quad -2\frac{1}{4}$

7. $7\frac{15}{16} - 2\frac{4}{8}$

8. $6\frac{1}{3} - 4\frac{5}{6}$

9. $3\frac{1}{5} - 1\frac{9}{10}$

Write >, <, or = for each ◯.

10. $7 - 3\frac{4}{9} \bigcirc 8\frac{1}{2} - 3\frac{1}{6}$

11. $9\frac{2}{5} - 1\frac{4}{6} \bigcirc 10 - 2\frac{4}{15}$

12. $6\frac{3}{8} - 5\frac{3}{4} \bigcirc 5\frac{1}{4} - 3\frac{5}{8}$

13. $8\frac{3}{4} - 3\frac{4}{5} \bigcirc 5\frac{1}{3} - 1\frac{5}{6}$

Problem Solving

Show Your Work

15. Zack has $3\frac{1}{4}$ ft of wood. Lance has $1\frac{3}{4}$ ft of wood. Zack cut a $\frac{7}{8}$ ft piece from his wood and gave it to Lance. Who has more wood now? Explain.

Use with text pages 274–276.

Explore Addition and Subtraction With Decimals

Find 0.37 + 0.09.

Step 1: Change the decimals to fractions.	**Step 2:** Add the fractions.	**Step 3:** Write the sum as a decimal.
$0.37 = \frac{37}{100}$ $0.09 = \frac{9}{100}$	$\frac{37}{100} + \frac{9}{100} = \frac{46}{100}$	$\frac{46}{100} = 0.46$

Change each decimal to a fraction. Model each addition and subtraction. Write each sum as a decimal.

1. 0.18 + 0.5

_____

2. 0.29 + 0.68

_____

3. 0.4 + 0.87

_____

4. 0.56 + 0.98

_____

5. 0.41 + 2.03

_____

6. 5.17 + 3.65

_____

7. 0.19 − 0.08

_____

8. 0.7 − 0.5

_____

9. 0.8 − 0.25

_____

10. 3.28 − 1.46

_____

11. 2.5 − 1.72

_____

12. 5.8 − 4.9

_____

Problem Solving

Show Your Work

13. Paul jogged 3.25 miles, Rick jogged $3\frac{1}{3}$ miles, and Sean jogged $3\frac{1}{8}$ miles. List the boys from least to greatest distance jogged. Tell how you found your answer.

_____

Use with text pages 282–283.

Add Decimals

Find 3.8 + 0.95.

| **Step 1:** Use the decimal points to line up the addends. Add zeros as needed.

3.**80**
+0.95 | **Step 2:** Add the hundredths.

3.80
+0.95
5 | **Step 3:** Add the tenths.

1
3.80
+0.95
75 | **Step 4:** Add the ones. Align the decimal point in the sum with the decimal point in the addends.

1
3.80
+0.95
4.75 |

Add. Use a calculator to check.

1. $12.42
   + 9.79

2.   9.1
   +5.88

3.   7.11
   +6.93

4.   6.13
   +45.2

5.   1.08
   +36.94

6.   6.2
   +74.75

7. 12.3 + 4.07

8. 26.4 + 0.005

9. 1.004 + 32.7

_____

_____

_____

10. 8.1 + 54.06 + 0.002

11. 5.72 + 0.108 + 93.25

12. 8.004 + 0.9 + 12.3

_____

_____

_____

Problem Solving

Show Your Work

13. Maxine has 4.5 m of wire. She uses 1.75 m for each floral wreath she makes. Does Maxine have enough wire to make three wreaths? Explain your answer.

_____

Use with text pages 284–285.

Subtract Decimals

Find 46.2 − 8.75.

| **Step 1:** Use the decimal points to line up the digits. Add zeros as needed.

46.20
− 8.75 | **Step 2:** Subtract the hundredths.

$\overset{110}{46.2\cancel{0}}$
− 8.75
5 | **Step 3:** Subtract the tenths.

$\overset{5\ 11}{4\cancel{6}.\cancel{2}0}$
− 8.75
45 | **Step 4:** Subtract the ones and tens. Write the decimal point in the answer.

$\overset{315}{\cancel{4}\cancel{6}.20}$
− 8.75
37.45 |

Subtract. Add to check your answer.

1. 7.3
    −1.5

2. 8.4
    −6.6

3. $23.55
    −   8.70

4. 11.4
    − 6.32

5. 3.08
    −0.946

6. 24.8
    − 7.005

7. 9.1 − 2.48

8. 6.04 − 3.9

9. $10 − 4.89

_____

_____

_____

10. 6.7 − 3.112

11. 11.4 − 3.3

12. $15.22 − 12.67

_____

_____

_____

Problem Solving

13. Tony bought two notebooks at $1.89 each. He paid for the notebooks with a $20 bill. How much change did he get?

Show Your Work

_____

Use with text pages 286–288.

Estimate Decimal Sums and Differences

Ways to Estimate 8.217 − 3.5		
Round to nearest whole number	**Front-end Estimation**	**Round to tenths**

8.217   8
−3.5   −4
         4
	8.217 8
	−3.5 −3
	         5
		8.217 8.2
		−3.5 −3.5
		         4.7

Estimate each sum or difference to the nearest tenth.

1. $0.548 + 0.356$ **2.** $0.721 + 0.894$ **3.** $0.155 + 0.426$ **4.** $0.659 + 0.121$

_____   _____   _____   _____

5. $0.793 - 0.518$ **6.** $0.409 - 0.316$ **7.** $0.564 - 0.293$ **8.** $0.917 - 0.462$

_____   _____   _____   _____

Estimate each sum or difference to the nearest whole number.

9. $5.16 + 7.8$ **10.** $21.8 + 6.33$ **11.** $3.05 + 41.749$ **12.** $16.08 + 7.4$

_____   _____   _____   _____

13. $62.9 - 45.13$ **14.** $17.6 - 13.2$ **15.** $31.5 - 19.1$ **16.** $4.26 - 0.978$

_____   _____   _____   _____

Problem Solving

Show Your Work

17. Nancy said that $23.5 - 7.2$ is about 31. Do you agree with her? Tell why or why not.

_____

Use with text pages 290–291.

Problem-Solving Decision:
Choose a Method

Ask Yourself

Understand What facts do I know?

Plan Should I use mental math?
Do I need to use pencil and paper?
Does it make sense to use a calculator?

Solve Which operation will I use to solve the problem?

Look Back Did I solve the problem?
Is my answer reasonable?

Solve. Explain which method you used.

Show Your Work

1. Ross ran a mile in 6.28 minutes to win a race. Don finished second with a time of 6.55 minutes. How much faster was Ross than Don?

   _____

2. Clark ran in the same race. His time was 1.37 minutes more than Ross's time. How long did it take Clark to run the mile?

   _____

3. On their new track shoes, Randy's shoe laces are 12.5 in. long, and Sarah's shoe laces are 13.75 in. long. How much longer are Sarah's shoe laces?

   _____

Use with text pages 292–293.

Model Multiplication

Find $\frac{1}{3} \times \frac{3}{4}$.

Use a Model to Multiply Fractions

Step 1: Draw a square.

Step 2: Use horizontal lines to separate it into thirds.

Step 3: Use vertical lines to separate it into fourths.

Step 4: Shade and label $\frac{1}{3}$ of the square.

Step 5: Shade and label $\frac{3}{4}$ of the square.

Step 6: Count the parts that are shaded twice. $\frac{1}{3} \times \frac{3}{4} = \frac{3}{12}$ or $\frac{1}{4}$

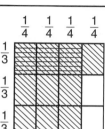

Write the equation represented by each model. Write the answer in simplest form.

1.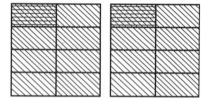

_____

2.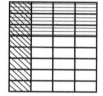

_____

3.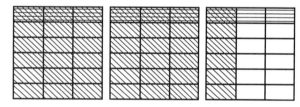

_____

4.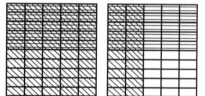

_____

Use models to find each product. Write the answer in simplest form.

5. $4 \times \frac{1}{8}$

_____

6. $1\frac{3}{4} \times \frac{2}{3}$

_____

7. $2\frac{1}{2} \times \frac{1}{3}$

_____

8. $6 \times \frac{3}{4}$

_____

Problem Solving

Show Your Work

9. Jane had $1\frac{1}{2}$ yards of cloth. She cut it into fourths. What is the size of one piece?

_____

Use with text pages 310–313.

Multiply Fractions

Different Ways to Find $\frac{2}{3}$ of $\frac{6}{8}$	
Way 1: Multiply, then simplify.	**Way 2:** Simplify, then multiply.
$\frac{2}{3} \times \frac{6}{8} = \frac{2 \times 6}{3 \times 8} = \frac{12}{24}$	$\frac{2}{3} \times \frac{6}{8} = \frac{\overset{1}{2} \times \overset{2}{6}}{\underset{1}{3} \times \underset{1}{2} \times 4} = \frac{2}{4}$
$\frac{12}{24} \div \frac{12}{12} = \frac{1}{2}$	$\frac{2 \div 2}{4 \div 2} = \frac{1}{2}$

Multiply. Write your answer in simplest form.

1. $\frac{1}{6} \times \frac{2}{3}$

2. $\frac{1}{8} \times 3$

3. $\frac{4}{9} \times \frac{3}{7}$

4. $\frac{2}{5} \times \frac{3}{5}$

_____   _____   _____   _____

5. $\frac{3}{4} \times \frac{5}{6}$

6. $\frac{1}{10} \times 5$

7. $\frac{4}{7} \times \frac{1}{4}$

8. $6 \times \frac{2}{3}$

_____   _____   _____   _____

9. $12 \times \frac{2}{3}$

10. $\frac{2}{5} \times \frac{1}{2}$

11. $\frac{8}{9} \times \frac{4}{5}$

12. $\frac{5}{6} \times 4$

_____   _____   _____   _____

Problem Solving

Show Your Work

13. Laurence owns 20 balls. $\frac{4}{5}$ of the balls are larger than a baseball, and $\frac{1}{2}$ of those are soccer balls. How many soccer balls does Laurence own?

_____

Use with text pages 314–315.

Multiply With Mixed Numbers

Find $3\frac{1}{3} \times \frac{3}{5}$.

Step 1: Write the mixed number as an improper fraction.	**Step 2:** Use common factors to simplify. Then multiply.	**Step 3:** Simplify. $\frac{2}{1} = 2$
$3\frac{1}{3} = \frac{10}{3}$	$\frac{10}{3} \times \frac{3}{5} = \frac{10 \times 3^1}{_{1}3 \times 5} = \frac{10 \times 1}{1 \times 5} = \frac{10}{5} = \frac{2}{1}$	$3\frac{1}{3} \times \frac{3}{5} = 2$

Multiply. Write each product in simplest form.

1. $1\frac{1}{5} \times \frac{3}{4}$

2. $2\frac{1}{8} \times \frac{1}{4}$

3. $3\frac{1}{6} \times \frac{2}{5}$

4. $\frac{4}{5} \times 2\frac{1}{2}$

_____   _____   _____   _____

5. $1\frac{3}{8} \times \frac{4}{5}$

6. $2\frac{1}{5} \times \frac{3}{7}$

7. $3\frac{1}{4} \times \frac{8}{9}$

8. $\frac{4}{7} \times 2\frac{3}{4}$

_____   _____   _____   _____

9. $1\frac{2}{5} \times \frac{1}{4}$

10. $\frac{1}{6} \times 3\frac{1}{3}$

11. $\frac{5}{9} \times 3\frac{2}{3}$

12. $5\frac{1}{2} \times \frac{4}{7}$

_____   _____   _____   _____

Problem Solving

Show Your Work

13. Kylie uses $1\frac{1}{2}$ cups of sugar for each batch of cookies she makes. How much sugar does she need to make 5 batches of cookies?

_____

Use with text pages 316–318.

Model Division

Find $9 \div \frac{1}{3}$.

Step 1: Draw 9 whole circles.

Step 2: Separate each circle into thirds.

Step 3: Count how many thirds are in
9 circles. $9 \div \frac{1}{3} = 27$

Write the equation represented by each model. Write the answer in simplest form.

1.

_____

2.

_____

3.

_____

4.

_____

Divide. Check your answers.

5. $\frac{3}{5} \div \frac{1}{5}$

6. $\frac{5}{8} \div \frac{1}{8}$

7. $\frac{7}{10} \div \frac{1}{10}$

8. $\frac{5}{6} \div \frac{1}{6}$

_____ _____ _____ _____

9. $\frac{10}{12} \div \frac{2}{12}$

10. $\frac{4}{5} \div \frac{2}{5}$

11. $\frac{9}{10} \div \frac{3}{10}$

12. $\frac{6}{8} \div \frac{2}{8}$

_____ _____ _____ _____

Problem Solving

Show Your Work

13. Compare $4 \div \frac{1}{8}$ and $8 \div \frac{1}{4}$. Use a model
to help explain your answer if necessary.

_____

Use with text pages 320–321.

Divide Fractions

Find $\frac{2}{3} \div \frac{6}{11}$.

Step 1: Rewrite as a multiplication problem using the reciprocal of the divisor.

$$\frac{2}{3} \div \frac{6}{11} = \frac{2}{3} \times \frac{11}{6}$$

Step 2: Find the product. Reduce if needed.

$$\frac{2}{3} \times \frac{11}{6} = \frac{22}{18} = 1\frac{2}{9}$$

Divide. Write each answer in simplest form.

1. $15 \div \frac{2}{3}$

2. $\frac{5}{8} \div \frac{5}{6}$

3. $\frac{3}{4} \div \frac{1}{3}$

4. $\frac{1}{2} \div \frac{7}{8}$

_____ _____ _____ _____

5. $10 \div 15$

6. $9 \div \frac{2}{3}$

7. $\frac{4}{5} \div \frac{1}{10}$

8. $\frac{11}{12} \div \frac{1}{4}$

_____ _____ _____ _____

9. $20 \div \frac{1}{2}$

10. $8 \div 12$

11. $\frac{3}{5} \div \frac{4}{7}$

12. $5 \div 7$

_____ _____ _____ _____

Problem Solving

Show Your Work

13. One-fourth of the students in the fifth grade play baseball. If 30 students play baseball, how many students are in the fifth grade?

_____

Use with text pages 322–323.

Divide Mixed Numbers

Find $3\frac{1}{3} \div 1\frac{1}{2}$.

Step 1: Write the mixed numbers as improper fractions.	$3\frac{1}{3} \div 1\frac{1}{2} = \frac{10}{3} \div \frac{3}{2}$
Step 2: Rewrite as a multiplication problem using the reciprocal of the divisor.	$\frac{10}{3} \times \frac{2}{3} =$
Step 3: Multiply. Simplify if needed.	$\frac{10}{3} \times \frac{2}{3} = \frac{20}{9} = 2\frac{2}{9}$

Divide. Write each quotient in simplest form.

1. $\frac{1}{3} \div 2\frac{1}{3}$ **2.** $\frac{5}{6} \div 1\frac{5}{6}$ **3.** $\frac{1}{2} \div 3\frac{1}{4}$ **4.** $1\frac{2}{5} \div 1\frac{3}{5}$

_____   _____   _____   _____

5. $\frac{1}{5} \div 3\frac{4}{5}$ **6.** $\frac{2}{3} \div 1\frac{1}{9}$ **7.** $\frac{3}{4} \div 1\frac{1}{2}$ **8.** $2\frac{1}{3} \div 1\frac{1}{6}$

_____   _____   _____   _____

9. $\frac{7}{8} \div 2\frac{3}{4}$ **10.** $\frac{5}{7} \div 2\frac{1}{2}$ **11.** $\frac{3}{5} \div 3\frac{1}{5}$ **12.** $\frac{4}{9} \div 5\frac{1}{3}$

_____   _____   _____   _____

Problem Solving

Show Your Work

13. Taylor collected $4\frac{1}{3}$ gallons of rain water and used $2\frac{1}{2}$ gallons to water her indoor plants. What fraction of the water she collected did she use to water the plants?

_____

Use with text pages 324–326.

Problem-Solving Decision: Choose the Operation

	Ask Yourself
Understand	What facts do I know?
Plan	What key words are in the problem?
Solve	Which operation will I use to solve the problem?
Look Back	Did I solve the problem? Is my answer reasonable?

Show Your Work

1. Theo's bedroom measures $12\frac{3}{4}$ ft by $9\frac{2}{3}$ ft. What is the difference between the length and width of the room?

   _____

2. Theo wants some wallpaper for his room. One wallpaper originally cost $8 a roll. Now it is on sale for $\frac{3}{4}$ the regular price. If Theo buys 5 rolls, how will much he pay?

   _____

3. Another wallpaper regularly costs $6 a roll. But if Theo buys 9 rolls, he will get $\frac{1}{3}$ off the regular price of each roll. How much will 9 rolls cost Theo?

   _____

4. The amount that Theo spent buying wallpaper in Problem 3 was $\frac{2}{3}$ of the total that both Theo and his parents spent altogether. How much did Theo and his parents spend shopping?

   _____

Use with text pages 328–329.

Explore Multiplication

Find $\frac{1}{4}$ of 1.2.

Step 1: Change 1.2 to a mixed number.	**Step 2:** Write the mixed number as an improper fraction.	**Step 3:** Multiply. Simplify, if needed.
$1.2 = 1\frac{2}{10}$ or $1\frac{1}{5}$	$1\frac{1}{5} = \frac{6}{5}$	$\frac{1}{4} \times \frac{6}{5} = \frac{6}{20} = \frac{3}{10}$

Use models or fractions to multiply. Write each product as a decimal.

1. 0.3×0.6

_____

2. 0.9×0.6

_____

3. 1.4×0.8

_____

4. 2.5×0.4

_____

5. 1.3×0.7

_____

6. 1.7×0.2

_____

7. 0.7×0.7

_____

8. 0.5×0.8

_____

9. 2.2×0.3

_____

10. 3.1×0.4

_____

11. 2.6×0.2

_____

12. 1.7×0.9

_____

Problem Solving

Show Your Work

13. Lydia worked 6.5 hours on Saturday and 3.25 hours on Sunday. Rafael worked twice as long as Lydia did. How long did Lydia and Rafael work altogether?

_____

Use with text pages 334–335.

Multiply Whole Numbers and Decimals

Multiply 4 × $1.89 = *s*.

Step 1: Estimate the product by rounding to the nearest whole number.	**Step 2:** Multiply. Ignore the decimal point.	**Step 3:** Insert the decimal point in the product.
4 × $2 = $8	$$\begin{array}{r} 189 \\ \times\ \ 4 \\ \hline 756 \end{array}$$	$1.89 → 2 decimal places × 4 → 0 decimal places $7.56 → 2 decimal places **Step 4:** Compare your answer with your estimate. $7.56 is close to 8. The answer is reasonable.

Find each product.

1. 5 × 2.2 _____

2. 3 × 0.12 _____

3. 2.75 × 7 _____

4. 12.5 × 4 _____

5. 8 × 4.2 _____

6. 14.1 × 2 _____

7. 7.6 × 3 _____

8. 9 × 3.9 _____

9. 5.2 × 7 _____

10. 3.172 × 5 _____

11. 14 × 0.28 _____

12. 17 × 9.5 _____

Problem Solving

Show Your Work

13. Last week, Felicia worked 4.5 hours on both Monday and Wednesday. She worked 6.5 hours on both Tuesday and Thursday. If she earns $7.50 an hour, how much did Felicia earn last week?

_____

Use with text pages 336–337.

Estimate Products

Ways to Estimate 228 × 0.77		
Round the numbers.	**Round to lesser numbers.**	**Use fractions.**
228 rounds to 200	228 rounds to 200	228 is about 200
0.77 rounds to 0.8	0.77 rounds to 0.7	0.77 is about $\frac{3}{4}$
$200 \times 0.8 = 160$	$200 \times 0.7 = 140$	$\frac{3}{4}$ of 200 is 150

Estimate each product.

1. 13×0.47

2. 5.96×3

3. 4×2.89

_____ _____ _____

4. 3×3.98

5. 9.87×12

6. 3.075×15

_____ _____ _____

7. 4.46×3

8. 1.52×23

9. 5×3.7

_____ _____ _____

10. 0.124×8

11. $\$4.79 \times 14$

12. $\$2.17 \times 6$

_____ _____ _____

Problem Solving

Show Your Work

13. Melissa is renting chairs for a party. Each chair rents for $2.19. About how much will it cost Melissa to rent 21 chairs?

_____

Use with text pages 338–339.

Multiply Decimals

Find 0.7 × 0.3.

Step 1: Multiply. Ignore the decimal points.

$$\begin{array}{r} 7 \\ \times 3 \\ \hline 21 \end{array}$$

Step 2: Place the decimal point in the product.

0.7	1 decimal place
×0.3	1 decimal place
0.21	2 decimal places

Multiply.

1. 0.7 × 0.2   **2.** 0.9 × 0.3   **3.** 0.32 × 0.5

_____   _____   _____

4. 0.3 × 6.2   **5.** 1.25 × 4.7   **6.** 0.6 × 5.4

_____   _____   _____

7. 2.65 × 0.29   **8.** 1.52 × 23   **9.** 1.57 × 6.6

_____   _____   _____

Compare. Write >, <, or =.

10. 0.4 × 6.1 ◯ 12.2 × 0.2   **11.** 3.5 × 1.7 ◯ 4.6 × 1.8

12. 0.9 × 5.6 ◯ 2.2 × 1.7   **13.** 0.4 × 3.8 ◯ 7.6 × 0.2

Problem Solving

Show Your Work

14. Jerome bought 1.4 pounds of string beans for $0.85 per pound. How much did he pay for string beans?

_____

Use with text pages 340–342.

Name _____ Date _____

Zeros in the Product

Find 0.02 × 0.04.

Step 1: Multiply. Ignore the decimal points.	**Step 2:** Place the decimal point in the product.
0.02 ×0.04 8	0.02 2 decimal places ×0.04 2 decimal places 0.0008 4 decimal places

Multiply.

1. 0.07
× 0.2

2. 0.03
× 0.9

3. 0.005
× 0.3

4. 0.002
× 0.08

5. 0.006
× 0.09

6. 0.025
× 0.7

7. 0.04
×0.01

8. 0.03
× 0.5

9. 0.051 × 0.06

10. 0.009 × 0.04

11. 0.08 × 0.005

12. 0.6 × 0.001

Problem Solving

Show Your Work

13. In the Turtle Trot race, a turtle travels at the rate of 0.09 miles per hour. How far will the turtle travel in 0.40 hours?

_____

Use with text pages 344–345.

Problem-Solving Decision:
Reasonable Answers

Ask Yourself

Understand	What is the problem?
	What facts do I know?
Plan	Which operation will I use to solve the problem?
Solve	Are my calculations correct?
Look Back	Did I solve the problem?
	Is my answer reasonable?

Solve. Explain why the answer is reasonable or unreasonable.

Show Your Work

1. Alvin earns $80. He plans to put 0.4 of
   that money in the bank and give his
   mother 0.2 of it. Alvin figures he will
   have $55 left over. Is he correct?

   _____

2. Alvin wants to buy a new video game
   system that costs $299. He plans to save
   $28.50 a week for the system. Alvin
   rounded the numbers to estimate how
   long it will take him to buy the system.
   He says he will have enough money after
   10 weeks. Is he correct?

   _____

88

Explore Division With Decimals

Find 8 ÷ 0.25.

Step 1: Write 8 and 0.25 as fractions. $8 \div \frac{1}{4}$

Step 2: Draw 8 circles to model 8 wholes.   ○○○○○○○○

Step 3: Separate each whole into four equal parts.   ⊕⊕⊕⊕⊕⊕⊕⊕

Step 4: Count the number of $\frac{1}{4}$s in all 8 wholes. $8 \div \frac{1}{4} = 32$

Model the division and write the quotient in decimal form.

1. $6 \div 0.25$ **2.** $9 \div 0.5$ **3.** $4 \div 0.4$ **4.** $7 \div 0.2$

_____   _____   _____   _____

5. $12 \div 0.4$ **6.** $3 \div 0.2$ **7.** $8 \div 0.5$ **8.** $2 \div 0.1$

_____   _____   _____   _____

9. $5 \div 0.2$ **10.** $6 \div 0.25$ **11.** $4 \div 0.2$ **12.** $8 \div 0.2$

_____   _____   _____   _____

Problem Solving

Show Your Work

13. A machine makes 24 donuts every 0.25 hour. At this rate, how many donuts are made in two hours?

_____

Use with text pages 352–353.

Estimate Quotients

Estimate 71 ÷ 0.28.

Step 1: Change the decimal to an equivalent unit fraction.	**Step 2:** Change the dividend to a compatible number.	**Step 3:** Estimate the number of fourths in 70. The quotient will be about 280.
0.28 is close to 0.25 $0.25 = \frac{1}{4}$	71 is close to 70	$70 \div \frac{1}{4} = 280$

Estimate each quotient.

1. 64 ÷ 0.48   **2.** 18.3 ÷ 0.31   **3.** 17 ÷ 0.19   **4.** 5.4 ÷ 0.21

_____   _____   _____   _____

5. 11.9 ÷ 0.12   **6.** 7.1 ÷ 0.214   **7.** 9.6 ÷ 0.53   **8.** 43.1 ÷ 0.492

_____   _____   _____   _____

9. 5.7 ÷ 0.32   **10.** 11.66 ÷ 0.2   **11.** 4.13 ÷ 0.802   **12.** 9 ÷ 0.247

_____   _____   _____   _____

Problem Solving

Show Your Work

13. The Hawks soccer team has won 0.2 of the games they've played. If the team has won 2 games, how many games have the Hawks played?

_____

Use with text pages 354–355.

Name _____ Date _____

Multiply and
Divide by Powers of 10

$0.0009 \times 10^1 = 0.009$	$78 \div 10^1 = 7.8$
$0.0009 \times 10^2 = 0.09$	$78 \div 10^2 = 0.78$
$0.0009 \times 10^3 = 0.9$	$78 \div 10^3 = 0.078$
$0.0009 \times 10^4 = 9$	$78 \div 10^4 = 0.0078$

Multiply or divide using patterns.

1. 45.8×10^2 **2.** $8.3 \div 10^1$ **3.** 0.755×10^3 **4.** $0.66 \div 10^2$

_____   _____   _____   _____

5. 1.624×10^3 **6.** $9.21 \div 10^1$ **7.** 0.38×10^2 **8.** $57.9 \div 10^1$

_____   _____   _____   _____

9. $2{,}615 \times 10^1$ **10.** $1.52 \div 10^1$ **11.** 3.73×10^2 **12.** $9{,}800 \div 10^3$

_____   _____   _____   _____

Problem Solving

Show Your Work

13. The distance between two stars is 3.45×10^3 miles. What is the distance expressed in standard form?

_____

Use with text pages 356–357.

Divide a Decimal by a Whole Number

Find 4.2 ÷ 7.

$\begin{array}{r} 6 \\ 7\overline{)42} \\ -42 \\ \hline 0 \end{array}$	**Step 1:** Divide the dividend, disregarding the decimal point.	$\begin{array}{r} 0.6 \\ 7\overline{)4.2} \\ -4.2 \\ \hline 0 \end{array}$	**Step 2:** Place a decimal point in the quotient above the decimal point in the dividend.

Divide and check.

1. $9\overline{)8.1}$ **2.** $5\overline{)5.75}$ **3.** $7\overline{)18.2}$ **4.** $6\overline{)0.012}$

5. $2.4 \div 3$ **6.** $0.56 \div 8$ **7.** $21.06 \div 9$ **8.** $7.5 \div 5$

_____   _____   _____   _____

9. $4\overline{)25.92}$ **10.** $2\overline{)6.32}$ **11.** $7\overline{)3.22}$ **12.** $8\overline{)1.68}$

Problem Solving

Show Your Work

13. A sailboat travels 24.9 miles in 3 hours. What is its average speed in miles per hour?

_____

Use with text pages 358–360.

Write Zeros in the Dividend

Find 8.5 ÷ 2.

$$
\begin{array}{r}
4\,2 \\
2\overline{)8.5} \\
-8 \\
\hline
0\,5 \\
-0\,4 \\
\hline
1
\end{array}
$$

Step 1: Divide as though the dividend were a whole number.

$$
\begin{array}{r}
4.25 \\
2\overline{)8.50} \\
-8 \\
\hline
0\,5 \\
-0\,4 \\
\hline
10 \\
-10 \\
\hline
0
\end{array}
$$

Step 2: Write a 0 in hundredths place. Continue dividing. Put a decimal point in the quotient above the decimal point in the dividend.

Divide. Check using a calculator or estimation.

1. $2\overline{)6.9}$

2. $4\overline{)50}$

3. $5\overline{)4.7}$

4. $8\overline{)92}$

5. 8.6 ÷ 4

6. 18.6 ÷ 8

7. 5.44 ÷ 5

8. 14.1 ÷ 6

_____   _____   _____   _____

Compare. Write >, <, or = for each ◯.

9. 0.75 ÷ 6 ◯ 1.08 ÷ 8

10. 9.8 ÷ 4 ◯ 14.7 ÷ 6

11. 1.46 ÷ 4 ◯ 2.19 ÷ 6

12. 18 ÷ 8 ◯ 12.9 ÷ 6

Problem Solving

Show Your Work

13. Vera cut a board 87.4 cm long into 4 equal pieces. How long is each piece?

_____

Use with text pages 362–364.

Repeating Decimals

Change $\frac{7}{22}$ to a decimal.

Step 1: Divide until the quotient ends or repeats.

Step 2: Put a decimal point in the quotient directly over the decimal point in the dividend.

Step 3: Write a bar over the part of the quotient that repeats.

$$\frac{7}{22} = 0.3\overline{18}$$

$$
\begin{array}{r}
.31818 \\
22)\overline{7.00000} \\
-\ 66 \\
\hline
40 \\
-\ 22 \\
\hline
180 \\
-\ 176 \\
\hline
40 \\
-\ 22 \\
\hline
180 \\
-\ 176 \\
\hline
4
\end{array}
$$

Change each fraction to decimal form.

1. $\frac{8}{11}$

2. $\frac{7}{12}$

3. $\frac{4}{9}$

4. $\frac{10}{22}$

_____ _____ _____ _____

5. $\frac{20}{24}$

6. $\frac{21}{36}$

7. $\frac{2}{45}$

8. $\frac{7}{30}$

_____ _____ _____ _____

9. $\frac{2}{18}$

10. $\frac{5}{27}$

11. $\frac{11}{33}$

12. $\frac{13}{45}$

_____ _____ _____ _____

Problem Solving

13. Ryan has had 7 hits in his last 12 at bats. How much more or less than a 0.500 batting average does he have?

Show Your Work

_____

Use with text pages 366–367.

Divide a Decimal by a Decimal

Find 3.75 ÷ 1.5.

| **Step 1:** Multiply the divisor and dividend by the same power of 10 so that the divisor is a whole number.

1.5)3.75 ⟶ 15)37.5 | **Step 2:** Divide. Place a decimal point in the quotient over the decimal point in the dividend. | 2.5
15)37.5
− 30
7 5
− 7 5
0 |

Divide. Round to the nearest hundredth. Check that your answer is reasonable.

1. 2.4)9.984

2. 0.4)20.8

3. 0.4)0.28

4. 0.5)4.25

5. 0.2)5.6

6. 0.06)0.018

7. 7.2)25.2

8. 1.6)3.44

9. 3.6)20.88

10. 0.9)14.76

11. 0.8)5.76

12. 1.4)8.82

Problem Solving

13. An overseas phone call costs $7.44 for 24.8 minutes. What was the price per minute of the call?

_____

Show Your Work

Use with text pages 368–369.

Problem-Solving Application:
Decide How to Write the Quotient

Ask Yourself

Understand	What is the problem?
	What facts do I know?
Plan	Which operation will I use to solve the problem?
Solve	What does the remainder represent?
Look Back	Does my answer make sense?

Solve. Explain how you used each remainder.

Show Your Work

1. A scout troop is making a holiday display. The display contains 175 roses. The scouts will buy the flowers from a florist who sells roses in boxes of twelve. What is the fewest number of boxes the scouts should buy?

   _____

2. The scouts want to give their troop leader a gift that costs $48. If the 15 troop members split the cost evenly, how much will each person contribute?

   _____

Use with text pages 370–372.

Points, Lines, and Rays

Name each figure.

> ### Ask Yourself
> • Which letters do I use to name each figure?
> • Do I need to write the letters in a certain order?

1. R   S

_____

2. M   N

_____

3. •
  J

_____

4. P   Q

_____

Describe each pair of lines. Use symbols if possible.

5.

_____

6.

_____

Draw and label each figure.

7. Ray *BC*

_____

8. Point *Q*

_____

9. Line *RT*

_____

10. Ray *AB*

_____

11. Plane *XYZ*

_____

12. Line segment *CD*

_____

Problem Solving

13. Line *AB* is perpendicular to line *MN*. How many right angles are formed where the two lines meet?

_____

Show Your Work

Use with text pages 390–391.

Measure, Draw, and Classify Angles

> **Classifying Angles**
>
> **Right angle:**   the measure is equal to 90°
>
> **Acute angle:**   the measure is greater than 0° and less than 90°
>
> **Obtuse angle:**   the measure is greater than 90° and less than 180°
>
> **Straight angle:**   the measure is equal to 180°

In Exercises 1–4, use symbols to name each angle three different ways.

1.

_____

2.

_____

3.

_____

4.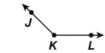

_____

Classify each angle as *acute*, *obtuse*, *straight*, or *right*.

5.

_____

6.

_____

7.

_____

Use a protractor to draw an angle having each measure.
Classify each angle as *right*, *acute*, *obtuse*, or *straight*.

8. 125°   **9.** 180°   **10.** 65°   **11.** 90°

_____   _____   _____   _____

Problem Solving

Show Your Work

12. How many right angles are needed to
make one straight angle?

_____

Use with text pages 392–395.

Name _____ Date _____

Triangles

Classifying Triangles	
By lengths of their sides:	**By their angle measures:**
Equilateral – all sides are the same length.	Right – one right angle
Isosceles – at least two sides are the same length.	Acute – all acute angles
Scalene – no sides are the same length.	Obtuse – one obtuse angle

Classify each triangle in two ways.

1. 6 cm / 6 cm, 6 cm

_____

2.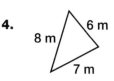
35 miles, 16 miles, 16 miles

_____

3.
7 in., 9 in., 11.4 in.

_____

4. 6 m, 8 m, 7 m

_____

Write an expression to represent _a_. Then find the value of _a_.

5. a, 55°

_____

6. 60°, 60°, a

_____

7. 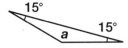 15°, 15°, a

_____

8. a, 25°, 35°

_____

Problem Solving

9. Can a right triangle contain a right angle and an obtuse angle? Explain.

Show Your Work

_____

   Use with text pages 396–397.

Name _____ Date _____

Congruence

Different Ways to Check for Congruence	
By tracing:	**By measuring:**
Trace one figure.	Use a ruler to measure the sides of the figures.
Place the tracing on top of the other figure.	Use a protractor to measure the angles of the figures.
If they are the same size and shape, the figures are congruent.	If the measurements are the same, the figures are congruent.

Use a ruler to measure the sides and a protractor to measure the angles of each figure. Mark the congruent sides and angles.

1.

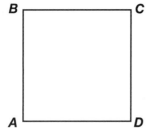

2.

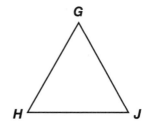

_____   _____

In the diagram △RST ≅ △VWU. Use the diagram to answer the questions. Explain your reasoning.

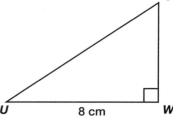

3. What is the length of side $\overline{VW}$?

_____

4. What is the measure of ∠V?

_____

5. What is the measure of ∠R?

_____

Problem Solving

6. If two squares have the same side lengths, are the squares necessarily congruent? Tell why or why not.

Show Your Work

_____

_____

                   Use with text pages 398–399.

Name _____ Date _____

Quadrilaterals and Other Polygons

Ask Yourself

- How many sides does the polygon have?
- Are any sides parallel?
- Are any sides congruent?
- Are any angles congruent?

Classify each polygon in as many ways as you can.

1.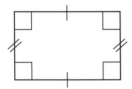

_____

2.

_____

3.

_____

4.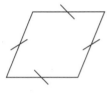

_____

Write *polygon* or *not a polygon* to classify each figure. If possible, find the measure of each missing angle.

5.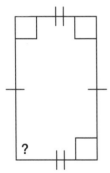

_____

6.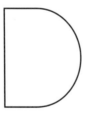

_____

Problem Solving

Show Your Work

7. If every square is a rectangle, is every rectangle also a square? Explain.

_____

101   **Use with text pages 400–402.**

Rotations, Reflections, and Translations

Transformation:	changes the position of a plane figure
Reflection:	figure flips over a line
Rotation:	figure turns around a point
Translation:	figure slides a given distance in a given direction

Tell whether each figure shows a translation, reflection, or rotation. If a figure shows a rotation, name the number of degrees of rotation.

1.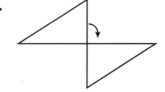

_____

2.

_____

3.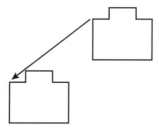

_____

Copy each figure on grid paper. Then complete the given transformations.

4.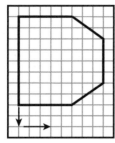

translation

5.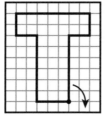

rotation of 90° clockwise

6.

reflection

Problem Solving

7. What happens when you translate a figure down three units, then up three units?

_____

Show Your Work

Use with text pages 404–406.

Problem-Solving Strategy:
Make a Model

Ask Yourself

Understand	What facts do I know?
Plan	Did I make a model? Does my model represent the pattern exactly?
Solve	Did I use transformations to test if the patterns fit together? Did I repeat the pattern enough so I could see if it tessellated? Did I tile the plane without gaps or overlaps?
Look Back	Did I solve the problem?

Make a model to solve each problem.

Show Your Work

1. Bill said that a regular hexagon will tessellate. Is he right or wrong? How do you know?

_____

2. Leah said this figure will tessellate. Do you agree with her? Explain.

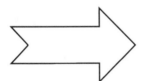

_____

3. Pedro said that this diamond will tessel- late. Do you agree with him? Tell why.

_____

Use with text pages 408–410.

Circles

Radius:	a segment that connects the center of a circle to any point on the circle
Diameter:	a segment that connects two points on the circle and passes through its center
Chord:	any segment that connects two points on the circle
Central angle:	an angle with its vertex at the center of the circle

Use symbols to identify the following parts of this circle.

1. chords

_____

2. radii

_____

3. central angles

_____

4. diameter

_____

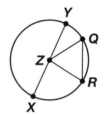

Classify each figure as radius, diameter, chord, or central angle. Indicate if more than one term applies.

5. $\overline{YX}$

_____

6. $\overline{QR}$

_____

7. $\angle YZQ$

_____

8. $\overline{RZ}$

_____

9. $\overline{QZ}$

_____

10. $\angle RZX$

_____

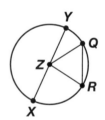

On a separate sheet of paper, construct a circle that contains all of the following.

11. center M

12. radius MN

13. diameter LMN

14. chord KL

15. central angle KML

16. chord JK

Problem Solving

17. What is the longest chord in a circle?

_____

Show Your Work

Use with text pages 412–413.

Name _____   Date _____

Symmetry

Ask Yourself

• Does this figure look exactly the way it did before the turn?

• How many degrees are in a full turn? a half turn? a quarter turn?

Trace each figure, and turn it. Write *yes* or *no* to tell if it has rotational symmetry. If it does, tell how many degrees you turned it.

1.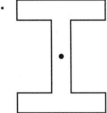

2.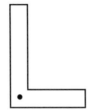

3.

_____   _____   _____

Trace each figure and fold it. Write *yes* or *no* to tell if it has line symmetry. If it does, write the number of lines of symmetry it has. Then sketch the figure, and its line(s) of symmetry.

4.

5.

6.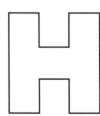

_____   _____   _____

Use a compass, a protractor, and another sheet of paper to draw these figures.

7. A figure with two lines of symmetry

8. A figure with rotational symmetry

9. A figure with no lines of symmetry

Problem Solving ──────────────────────

10. How many lines of symmetry does a circle have?

Show Your Work

_____

105   **Use with text pages 414–416.**

Name _____ Date _____

Perimeter

Formulas for Perimeter	
Perimeter of a square $P = 4s$	**Perimeter of a rectangle** $P = 2l + 2w$

Find the perimeter or the missing length.

1. _____
8 m
14 m

2. _____
6.5 ft
4.25 ft

3. _____
$2\frac{3}{4}$ ft
$2\frac{3}{4}$ ft

4. _____
$P = 22$ ft
7 ft

5.
6.5 yd $P = 26$ yd _____

6.
$P = 17.6$ m _____
3.6 m

Complete the chart below. Each figure in the chart is a regular figure with sides of 4 centimeters.

Regular Figure	Addition Expression	Multiplication Expression	Perimeter
7. triangle			
8. pentagon			
9. heptagon			

Problem Solving

Show Your Work

10. Mae's bedroom is in the shape of a rectangle that is 12 feet long and 9 feet wide. She is putting up a wallpaper border along all four walls of the room. The border is sold in two-yard packs. What is the least number of packs that Mae can buy?

_____

Use with text pages 422–423.

Problem-Solving Strategy:
Find a Pattern

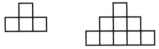

	Ask Yourself
Understand	What facts do I know?
Plan	What kinds of patterns can I look for?
Solve	Did I figure out how each shape in the pattern was different from the shape before it?
	Did I describe the pattern?
	Did I continue the pattern?
Look Back	How can I check the answer?

Use a pattern to solve each problem.

Show Your Work

1. Claudio made this pattern.

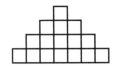

If the pattern continues, how many small squares
will be in the sixth shape?

_____

2. There are 12 flowers in the first row of a garden.
The second row has 20 flowers, the third row has
30 flowers, and the fourth row has 42 flowers.
How many flowers are likely in the sixth row?

_____

3. Find the next three figures that the star will be
in the same position as it is in the first shape.

_____

       Use with text pages 424–426.

Name _____ Date _____

Area of a Parallelogram

Formulas for Area	
Area of a rectangle $A = l \times w$	**Area of a parallelogram** $A = b \times h$

Find the area of each figure.

1.

5 m   6 m
12 m

_____

2.

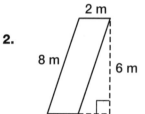

_____

3.

3 ft   4 ft
15 ft

_____

4.

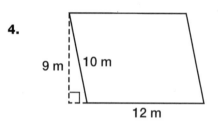

_____

5.

8 yd

13 yd

_____

6.

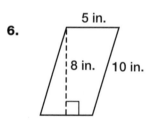

_____

Problem Solving

7. Identify the length and width of three different rectangles that have an area of 24cm².

_____

Show Your Work

108   **Use with text pages 428–430.**

Name _____ Date _____

Area of a Triangle

Find the area of a triangle with a base of 8 cm and a height of 6 cm.

$A = \frac{1}{2} \times b \times h$ $A = \frac{1}{2} \times 8 \times 6$ $A = 24 \text{ cm}^2$

Find the area of each triangle.

1.

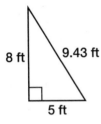

8 ft   9.43 ft

5 ft

_____

2. 2 m

8 m

_____

3.

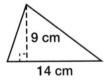

9 cm

14 cm

_____

4.

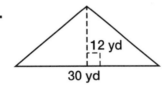

12 yd

30 yd

_____

5.

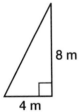

8 m

4 m

_____

6.

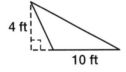

4 ft

10 ft

_____

Problem Solving

Show Your Work

7. A triangle has a base of 3.6 cm and an area of 22.32 cm². What is the height of this triangle?

_____

Use with text pages 432–433.

Name _____ Date _____

Perimeter and Area of Irregular Figures

Finding the Perimeter of an Irregular Figure	Finding the Area of an Irregular Figure
Step 1: Find any missing lengths.	**Step 1:** Divide the figure into simple figures.
Step 2: Add the lengths of all the sides.	**Step 2:** Use formulas to find the area of each simple figure.
	Step 3: Add the areas.

Find the perimeter and area of each figure. All intersecting sides meet at right angles.

1.

9 cm
3 cm
9 cm 5 cm
6 cm
4 cm

_____

2.

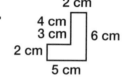

2 cm
4 cm
3 cm 6 cm
2 cm
5 cm

_____

3.

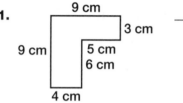

11 m
2 m
2 m
10 m 12 m
9 m

_____

4.

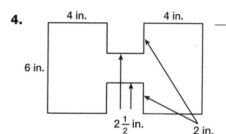

4 in. 4 in.
6 in.
$2\frac{1}{2}$ in. 2 in.

_____

5.

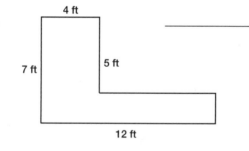

4 ft
7 ft 5 ft
12 ft

_____

6.

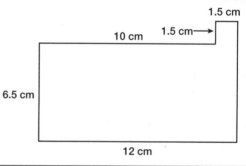

1.5 cm
10 cm 1.5 cm
6.5 cm
12 cm

_____

Problem Solving

7. Draw two irregular figures each with a perimeter of 20 inches.

_____

Show Your Work

Use with text pages 434–436.

Circumference of a Circle

How to Find Circumference of a Circle	
If you know the diameter *d*: $C = \pi d$	**If you know the radius *r*:** $C = 2\pi r$

Express each circumference as a fraction or mixed number in simplest form. Use $\frac{22}{7}$ for .

1. 9 m   _____

2. 14 m   _____

3. 10 in.   _____

4. $\frac{1}{4}$ m   _____

5. $2\frac{1}{2}$ ft   _____

6. $\frac{9}{7}$ yd   _____

Problem Solving

Show Your Work

7. The diameter of a circular watch face is 3 cm. What is the circumference of the watch face? Use $\frac{22}{7}$ for π.

_____

         Use with text pages 438–440.

Solid Figures

face:	a flat polygonal surface of a solid figure
edge:	line segment formed where two faces meet
vertex:	a point where three or more edges meet
prism:	a solid figure that has two parallel congruent bases that are polygons joined by rectangular faces
pyramid:	a solid figure that has one base that is a polygon and triangular faces that share a vertex

Name each solid figure. Then write the number of faces, vertices, and edges.

1. 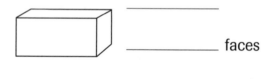 _____

_____ faces

_____ vertices

_____ edges

2. 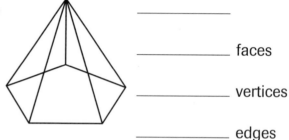 _____

_____ faces

_____ vertices

_____ edges

3. 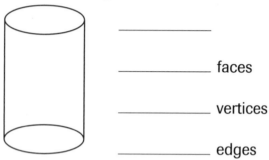 _____

_____ faces

_____ vertices

_____ edges

4. _____

_____ faces

_____ vertices

_____ edges

5. _____

_____ faces

_____ vertices

_____ edges

6. 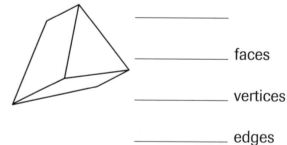 _____

_____ faces

_____ vertices

_____ edges

Problem Solving

Show Your Work

7. Alta traced the base of a solid figure. A square formed on her paper. What solid figures could she have traced?

_____

Use with text pages 446–447.

Two-Dimensional Views
of Solid Figures

Ask Yourself

• Which view can I use to tell how the bottom layer of cubes is arranged?

• How can I use the side and top views to help me visualize the rest of the figure?

**Use cubes to build a three-dimensional figure with these views. Then draw the
figure on triangular dot paper.**

1.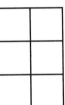

    Top View   Left Side View   Front View

2.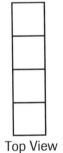

       Left Side View   Front View

    Top View

3.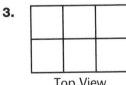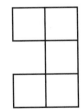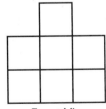

    Top View   Right Side View   Front View

Problem Solving

Show Your Work

4. When three cubes are lined up side by
side, and touching each other, how
many of the faces are hidden?

Use with text pages 448–449.

Nets

Predict what shape each net will make.

1. 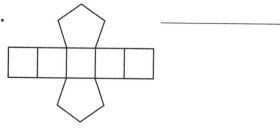 _____

2. 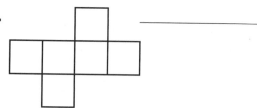 _____

3. 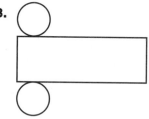 _____

4. 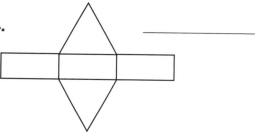 _____

Draw a net for each solid figure.

5.

6.

7.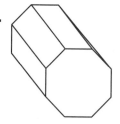

8.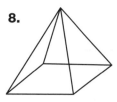

Problem Solving

9. Paula is making a model of a hexagonal prism. She will cut two-dimensional shapes from paper and tape them together. Identify the shapes Paula should cut to make her model.

_____

Show Your Work

Use with text pages 450–451.

Name _____ Date _____

Surface Area

Ask Yourself

• Which numbers do I multiply to find the surface area of each face?

• Which numbers do I add to find the surface area of the solid?

Determine the surface area of each solid figure.

1. _____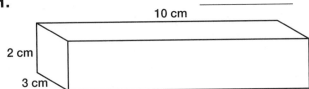

10 cm

2 cm

3 cm

2. _____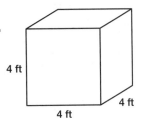

4 ft

4 ft

4 ft

3. _____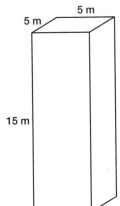

5 m

5 m

15 m

4. _____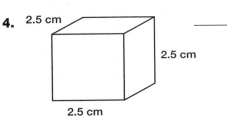

2.5 cm

2.5 cm

2.5 cm

2.5 cm

Copy and complete the table.

Length of One Side (s) of Cube	Area of One Face (f)	Surface Area of Cube (SA)
5. 3.5 cm		
6. 9 cm		
7. 15 cm		
8. 20 cm		

Problem Solving

9. What is the difference between a cube and a rectangular prism?

Show Your Work

_____

Use with text pages 452–454.

Name _____ Date _____

Problem-Solving Strategy: Solve a Simpler Problem

Ask Yourself

Understand What facts do I know?

Plan Did I use all the needed information?

Solve Did I solve a simpler problem first?

Look Back Did I solve the problem?
Is my answer reasonable?

Solve each problem by solving a simpler problem.

Show Your Work

1. How many squares can you find in the figure?

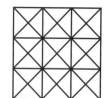

_____

2. A solid figure is 6 cubes wide, 6 cubes long, and 6 cubes high. The cube is made up of red and green cubes. There are twice as many green cubes as red cubes. How many red cubes does the figure contain?

_____

3. Josh built a tower with multi-colored blocks. As he built from the ground up, he used this pattern: red, yellow, yellow, blue. What color is the 32nd block in Josh's tower?

_____

4. Each of the 10 members of a School Board shook hands with every other member. How many handshakes were there?

_____

Use with text pages 456–458.

Name _____ Date _____

Volume

Formulas for Volume		
Volume of a Cube	**Volume of a Rectangular Prism**	**Volume of a Triangular Prism**
$V = s^3$	$V = l \times w \times h$	$V = \frac{1}{2}(l \times w \times h)$

Determine the volume of each solid figure.

1. 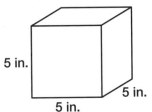 _____

5 in. 5 in. 5 in.

2. 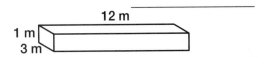 _____

12 m
1 m
3 m

3. 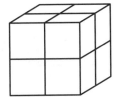 _____

4. 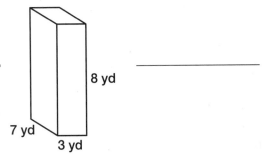 _____

8 yd
7 yd
3 yd

5. 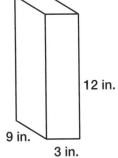 _____

12 in.
9 in.
3 in.

6. 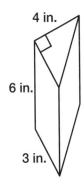 _____

4 in.
6 in.
3 in.

Problem Solving

7. Iris' lunchbox has a volume of 300 cubic inches. If its height is 10 in. and its width is 3 in., what is its length?

Show Your Work

_____

Use with text pages 460–463.

Problem-Solving Application:
Use Formulas

Ask Yourself	
Understand	What does the question ask me to find?
Plan	Which formulas do I need to use?
Solve	Did I choose the correct formulas?
	Did I substitute the correct numbers for the variables?
Look Back	Did I solve the problem?
	Is my answer reasonable?

Use formulas to solve Problems 1–3.

Show Your Work

1. Odessa needs to wrap a box that is 10 in. long, 6 in. wide, and 3 in. high. How much wrapping paper does she need?

   _____

2. Akio bought a storage cube that is 4.5 ft long, 4.5 ft wide, and 4.5 ft high. What is the maximum amount of storage space in the cube?

   _____

3. A new floor has been ordered for the school's rectangular lunchroom. The length of the lunchroom is twice its width. If the lunchroom is 32 ft wide, how many square feet of flooring were ordered?

   _____

Use with text pages 464–466.

Ratios

Ways to Write a Ratio		
Word form: 1 to 3	**Ratio form:** 1:3	**Fraction form:** $\frac{1}{3}$

Write each ratio three different ways.

Game Pieces	Number
Rectangles	6
Triangles	10
Parallelograms	9

1. all shapes to triangles

   _____

2. parallelograms to all shapes

   _____

3. rectangles to parallelograms

   _____

4. triangles to parallelograms

   _____

5. all shapes to rectangles

   _____

6. parallelograms to triangles

   _____

7. rectangles to triangles

   _____

8. triangles to all shapes

   _____

Problem Solving

Show Your Work

9. Natu has a bag of shapes. There are 5 squares, 9 triangles, and 7 circles. What is the ratio of circles to squares?

   _____

Use with text pages 484–485.

Equivalent Ratios

Different Ways to Find Equivalent Ratios	
Way 1: Multiply each term by the same number. $\dfrac{3}{9} = \dfrac{3 \times 2}{9 \times 2} = \dfrac{6}{18}$	**Way 2:** Divide each term by the same number. $\dfrac{3}{9} = \dfrac{3 \div 3}{9 \div 3} = \dfrac{1}{3}$

Write four equivalent ratios for each.

1. $\dfrac{2}{5}$ 2. 3:7   3. 2 to 9   4. $\dfrac{1}{6}$

_____ _____   _____ _____   _____ _____   _____ _____

_____ _____   _____ _____   _____ _____   _____ _____

5. 2:4   6. 4 to 7   7. $\dfrac{6}{5}$ 8. 5 to 8

_____ _____   _____ _____   _____ _____   _____ _____

_____ _____   _____ _____   _____ _____   _____ _____

Write each ratio in simplest form.

9. 16:24   10. 35 to 14   11. 20:15   12. 24 to 72

_____   _____   _____   _____

13. 42:14   14. 50 to 75   15. 30:45   16. 28 to 35

_____   _____   _____   _____

Complete each set of equivalent ratios.

17. $\dfrac{8}{3} = \dfrac{\square}{24}$ 18. $\dfrac{6}{21} = \dfrac{\square}{7}$ 19. $\dfrac{13}{52} = \dfrac{1}{\square}$

_____   _____   _____

Problem Solving

Show Your Work

20. Three copies of a book cost $20. Write an equivalent ratio to show the cost of 9 copies.

_____

Use with text pages 486–487.

Rates

Carey can purchase 6 cans of cat food for $2. How many cans of cat food can she purchase with $10?

Different Ways to Solve Problems Involving Rates

Way 1: Use equivalent ratios.

$$\overset{\times 5}{\frac{6}{2}} = \underset{\times 5}{\frac{30}{10}}$$

Way 2: Find the unit rate and multiply.

$$\frac{6}{2} = \frac{3}{1} \qquad \frac{3}{1} = \frac{3 \times 10}{1 \times 10} = \frac{30}{10}$$

Carey can purchase 30 cans of catfood.

Find the unit rate.

1. 150 miles in 3 hours

2. 63 yards in 9 minutes

3. $2,100 in 4 weeks

_____

_____

_____

4. $135 in 5 hours

5. 21 pages in 7 hours

6. 642 meters in 6 minutes

_____

_____

_____

7. 85 drivers in 17 minutes

8. 120 sales in 3 hours

9. 98 calls in 7 minutes

_____

_____

_____

Complete the unit rate.

10. 506 mi : 22 gal = _____ mi : 1 gal

11. $1.28 : 8 oz = _____¢ : 1 oz

12. 765 mi : 3 days = _____ mi : 1 day

13. $13.75 : 5 lbs = $_____ : 1 lb

14. $19.56 : 4 gal = $_____ : 1 gal

15. $31.50 : 9 tickets = $_____ : 1 ticket

Problem Solving

Show Your Work

16. Chris can assemble a tent in 4 minutes. How many minutes will it take him to assemble 6 tents?

_____

Use with text pages 488–490.

Proportions

Different Ways to Solve Problems Involving Proportions

Way 1: Use equivalent ratios.	**Way 2:** Use cross products.
$\dfrac{3}{7} = \dfrac{18}{\square}$	$\dfrac{3}{7} \diagup \dfrac{18}{n} = 3 \times n = 7 \times 18$
$\dfrac{3}{7} = \dfrac{3 \times 6}{7 \times 6} = \dfrac{18}{42}$	$\dfrac{3n}{3} = \dfrac{126}{3} \qquad n = 42$

Solve each proportion.

1. $\dfrac{2}{9} = \dfrac{8}{p}$ _____

2. $\dfrac{5}{7} = \dfrac{j}{56}$ _____

3. $\dfrac{m}{51} = \dfrac{1}{3}$ _____

4. $\dfrac{28}{r} = \dfrac{2}{3}$ _____

5. $\dfrac{45}{60} = \dfrac{3}{n}$ _____

6. $\dfrac{a}{12} = \dfrac{12}{144}$ _____

7. $\dfrac{27}{33} = \dfrac{t}{11}$ _____

8. $\dfrac{18}{b} = \dfrac{36}{44}$ _____

Write the cross products for each pair of ratios. Do the two ratios form a proportion? Write *yes* or *no*.

9. $\dfrac{9}{11}$ $\dfrac{35}{44}$ _____

10. $\dfrac{5}{4}$ $\dfrac{60}{48}$ _____

11. $\dfrac{13}{7}$ $\dfrac{52}{28}$ _____

12. $\dfrac{7}{9}$ $\dfrac{14}{18}$ _____

13. $\dfrac{42}{88}$ $\dfrac{6}{11}$ _____

14. $\dfrac{9}{21}$ $\dfrac{30}{70}$ _____

15. $\dfrac{25}{85}$ $\dfrac{5}{18}$ _____

16. $\dfrac{32}{56}$ $\dfrac{8}{14}$ _____

Problem Solving

Show Your Work

17. Suzu needs 24 boxes of juice for a party. A package of 3 boxes costs $0.99. Write and solve a proportion to find how much 24 boxes cost.

_____

Use with text pages 492–494.

Similar Figures and Scale Drawings

**Use 1 cm:10 m as a scale. Find the length of a wall in a
scale drawing if the actual wall is 120 m long.**

Step 1: Write a proportion.	**Step 2:** Solve a proportion.
$\dfrac{\text{length in drawing}}{\text{actual length}} \rightarrow \dfrac{1}{10} = \dfrac{n}{120}$	$\dfrac{1}{10} = \dfrac{n}{120}$ Use cross products.
	$1 \times 120 = 10n$
	$120 = 10n$
	$12 = n$
	12 cm is the length of the wall in the scaled drawing.

Use the scale 1 cm:3 m to find *n* in each case.

1. 7 cm in the drawing represents *n* m.

_____

2. 0.25 cm in the drawing represents *n* m.

_____

3. 0.5 cm in the drawing represents *n* m.

_____

4. 4.5 cm in the drawing represents *n* m.

_____

**Tell whether the rectangles in each pair are similar.
Explain your answers.**

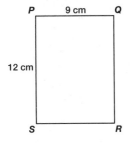
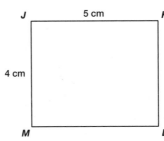

5. rectangle *JKLM* and rectangle *PQRS* _____

6. rectangle *PQRS* and rectangle *WXYZ* _____

7. rectangle *JKLM* and rectangle *WXYZ* _____

Problem Solving

Show Your Work

8. A map scale shows 1 cm:300 km.
What is the actual distance between
two towns that are 3.5 cm apart on
the map?

_____

Use with text pages 496–498.

Problem-Solving Decision:
Estimate or Exact Answer?

Ask Yourself

Understand   What question do I need to answer?

Plan   Can I use an estimate?
                 Do I need to find an exact answer?

Solve   Which operation will I use to solve the problem?

Look Back   Did I answer the question?

**Solve It. Tell whether you used an estimate or
an exact answer, and explain why.**

Show Your Work

1. A package of 15 stickers costs $2.29.
   A package of 50 stickers costs $6.59.
   Which is the better buy?

   _____

---

2. A 5-lb bag of oranges costs $1.89.
   An 8-lb bag of oranges costs $3.29.
   Which is the better buy?

   _____

---

3. Joy bought a package of six pairs of socks
   for $18.49. Later, she saw a package of
   four pairs of the same socks for $15.88.
   Did Joy get the better buy?

   _____

Use with text pages 500–501.

Understand Percent

Ways to Write a Percent (%)		
Sixty percent is written 60%.	$60\% = \frac{60}{100}$	$\frac{60}{100} = 0.60$ or 0.6

Write each ratio as a percent.

1. $\frac{87}{100}$

2. $\frac{56}{100}$

3. $\frac{29}{100}$

4. $\frac{17}{100}$

_____

_____

_____

_____

5. $\frac{8}{100}$

6. $\frac{16}{100}$

7. $\frac{38}{100}$

8. $\frac{65}{100}$

_____

_____

_____

_____

9. 75 parts out of 100

10. 5 parts out of 100

11. 30 parts out of 100

12. 9 parts out of 100

_____

_____

_____

_____

Write each percent as a ratio in simplest form.

13. 44%

14. 62%

15. 80%

16. 77%

_____

_____

_____

_____

17. 4%

18. 54%

19. 19%

20. 1%

_____

_____

_____

_____

Problem Solving

Show Your Work

21. How would you show 25% on a 10 × 10 grid?

_____

Use with text pages 506–507.

Relate Fractions, Decimals, and Percents

Ask Yourself

• Did I write each percent or decimal as a ratio with a second term of 100?

• Did I write each fraction in simplest form?

Copy and complete the table. Write each fraction in simplest form.

	Fraction	Decimal	Percent
1.			5%
2.		0.55	
3.	$\frac{3}{10}$		
4.		0.14	
5.	$\frac{23}{50}$		
6.			85%
7.		0.4	

Algebra Solve each equation for *n*.

8. $\frac{21}{n} = \frac{7}{10}$

9. $\frac{n}{50} = \frac{38}{100}$

10. $n\% = \frac{19}{20}$

11. $72\% = \frac{n}{25}$

_____   _____   _____   _____

12. $n\% = \frac{1}{50}$

13. $54\% = \frac{n}{100}$

14. $92\% = \frac{n}{25}$

15. $n\% = \frac{81}{100}$

_____   _____   _____   _____

Problem Solving

Show Your Work

16. There are 25 students in French class. Twelve of them are girls. What percent of the students are boys?

_____

Use with text pages 508–509.

Compare Fractions, Decimals, and Percents

Compare $\frac{7}{10}$, 46%, and 0.63 to find the greatest.

Way 1: Rewrite the fraction as a decimal.	**Way 2:** Think of the percent as a number of hundredths.	**Way 3:** Compare.
$\begin{array}{r} 0.7 \\ 10\overline{)7.0} \\ -\ 7.0 \\ \hline 0 \end{array}$	$46\% = \frac{46}{100} = 0.46$	$0.7 > 0.63 > 0.46$

Which is greatest?

1. $\frac{3}{5}$ 0.56 55%

_____

2. $\frac{3}{8}$ 0.38 35%

_____

3. $\frac{2}{9}$ 0.25 24%

_____

4. $\frac{8}{11}$ 0.7 71%

_____

5. $\frac{6}{7}$ 0.4 86%

_____

6. $\frac{2}{3}$ 0.62 65%

_____

Which is least?

7. $\frac{1}{10}$ 0.11 19%

_____

8. $\frac{7}{10}$ 0.63 47%

_____

9. $\frac{3}{4}$ 0.71 73%

_____

10. $\frac{2}{5}$ 0.42 41%

_____

11. $\frac{1}{2}$ 0.52 55%

_____

12. $\frac{19}{20}$ 58% 0.53

_____

Order each set from greatest to least.

13. $\frac{37}{50}$ 0.8 76%

_____

14. $\frac{1}{4}$ 0.31 27%

_____

15. $\frac{4}{5}$ 0.65 82%

_____

Problem Solving

Show Your Work

16. In an art class, 0.4 of the students are 9 years old, and $\frac{9}{20}$ are 10 years old. Fiften percent of the students in the class are 11 years old. Order the number of students by age from least to greatest.

_____

Use with text pages 510–512.

Find 10% of a Number

Find 10% of 75.

Way 1: Use a model.

100% of 75 = 75

10% | | | | | | | | |
n

To find n, divide 75 by 10.

$$75 \div 10 = 7.5$$

Way 2: Multiply by $\frac{1}{10}$.

$$\frac{1}{10} \times \frac{75}{1} = \frac{75}{10}$$

$$= 7.5$$

Way 3: Move the decimal point one place to the left to divide by 10.

$$75 \div 10 = 7.5$$

Find 10% of each number.

1. 78

2. 4

3. 0.27

4. 315

_____ _____ _____ _____

5. 19.75

6. 448.9

7. 641

8. 200.3

_____ _____ _____ _____

Find 20% of each number.

9. 70

10. 500

11. 6.28

12. 18

_____ _____ _____ _____

Estimate each percent of a number.

13. 21% of 403

14. 9% of 22

15. 48% of 92

16. 12% of 57

_____ _____ _____ _____

Problem Solving

Show Your Work

17. Tom went to the mall with $5.50. He spent 20% of the money on a soda. How much money is left?

_____

Use with text pages 514–515.

Percent of a Number

Different Ways to Find 55% of 60	
Way 1: Write the percent as a fraction and multiply. $55\% = \frac{55}{100}$ $= \frac{11}{20}$ $\frac{11}{20} \times \frac{60}{1} = \frac{33}{1}$ $= 33$	**Way 2:** Write the percent in decimal form and multiply. $55\% = 0.55$ $0.55 \times 60 = 33$

Solve by writing the percent as a fraction.

1. 20% of 85   **2.** 45% of 320   **3.** 50% of 47   **4.** 30% of 200

_____   _____   _____   _____

5. 60% of 150   **6.** 85% of 20   **7.** 50% of 82   **8.** 24% of 40

_____   _____   _____   _____

Solve by writing the percent as a decimal.

9. 29% of 50   **10.** 18% of 300   **11.** 75% of 21   **12.** 40% of 60

_____   _____   _____   _____

13. 70% of 120   **14.** 55% of 70   **15.** 32% of 80   **16.** 35% of 16

_____   _____   _____   _____

Solve. Use any method.

17. 12% of 60   **18.** 15% of 30   **19.** 58% of 90   **20.** 22% of 80

_____   _____   _____   _____

Problem Solving

Show Your Work

21. A toy car sells for $13.50. How much tax will be charged if the sales tax is 6% of the price?

_____

Use with text pages 516–518.

Problem-Solving Application:
Use Circle Graphs

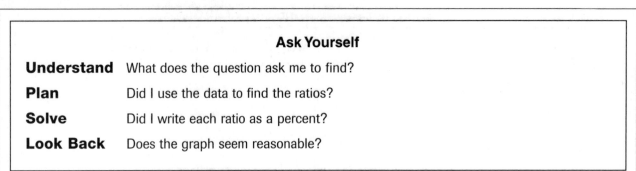

Ask Yourself

Understand   What does the question ask me to find?

Plan   Did I use the data to find the ratios?

Solve   Did I write each ratio as a percent?

Look Back   Does the graph seem reasonable?

Use the circle graph for Problems 1 and 2.

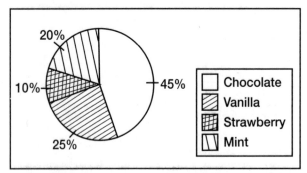

20%

10%

45%

25%

☐ Chocolate
▨ Vanilla
▦ Strawberry
⧄ Mint

Show Your Work

1. Hama asked 80 people to name their favorite
   flavor of ice cream. She displayed her results in
   a circle graph. How many people chose chocolate?

   _____

2. Based on Hama's results, how many people in
   a group of 250 would likely choose strawberry?

   _____

Use the table for Problem 3.

Ice Cream Shop Sales	
Cones	108
Sundaes	84
Milk Shakes	48

3. A total of 240 customers bought items at the
   Ice Cream Shop on July 5. Make a circle graph
   to display the data as percents.

         Use with text pages 520–522.

Make Choices

Different Ways to Find the Number of Choices		
Make an organized list.	**Make a tree diagram.**	**Multiply.**
juice, pancakes juice, cereal juice, eggs milk, pancakes milk, cereal milk, eggs	juice < pancakes / cereal / eggs milk < pancakes / cereal / eggs	drink choices × meal choices = total 2 × 3 = 6

You have one choice from each column. Make an organized list and a tree diagram to show all the possible choices.

1.

Outfits

Pants		**Tops**	
Tan	Black	White	Green
Blue		Red	Beige

2.

Activities

Morning	**Afternoon**
Swimming	Golf
Archery	Hiking
Canoeing	

3.

Frame Choices

Matte		**Frame**	
Blue	Red	Oak	Gold
White	Grey	Silver	Black
Green			

You have one choice from each category. Multiply to find the number of choices possible.

4. 5 types of pie, 3 types of ice cream

5. 6 meats, 4 types of bread

6. 5 beverages, 7 desserts

_____   _____   _____

Problem Solving

7. You can choose from 8 different exterior car colors and 4 different interior seat covering colors. How many possible combinations are there?

Show Your Work

_____

Use with text pages 528–529.

Name _____ Date _____

Probability Concepts

The probability of an event describes the likelihood the event will occur.

less likely   more likely

Impossible |—————————————————| Certain
          0   1
      Probability   Probability

As the probability of an event gets closer to 0, the event becomes less likely. As the probability of an event gets closer to 1, the event becomes more likely.

**You spin once on the spinner at the right.
Tell which event is less likely. If possible,
describe an event as impossible or certain.**

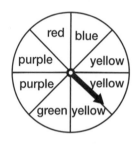

1. red or purple

_____

2. orange or brown

_____

3. yellow or purple

_____

4. green or any other color

_____

5. purple or blue

_____

6. green or orange

_____

7. silver or gold

_____

8. yellow or blue

_____

Problem Solving

9. A number cube has numbers 1 to 6. If
Mack tosses the number cube, what is
the probability that the event is 7?
Explain your answer.

Show Your Work

_____

Use with text pages 530–531.

Name _____ Date _____

Theoretical Probability

Finding Theoretical Probability

• How many outcomes are there?

• How many outcomes are favorable?

• Did I express the probability of an event as a ratio between the number of favorable outcomes and the total number of outcomes?

• Is the ratio in simplest form?

There are 16 shapes to be put in a bag. Use the bag of shapes for Problems 1–8. You picked one shape from the bag without looking. Find the theoretical probability of each event. Express the probability as a fraction in simplest form.

1. a black triangle

2. a square

_____

_____

3. any triangle or a black circle

4. a white square

5. a dotted shape

_____

_____

_____

6. a black or white circle

7. a white triangle

8. not a white square

_____

_____

_____

Suppose you toss a number cube that has sides labeled 1–6. Find the probability of each event.

9. a number less than 7

10. an odd number

11. a number that is greater than 4

_____

_____

_____

Problem Solving

12. Name an event that has a probability of $\frac{2}{7}$.

Show Your Work

_____

133

Use with text pages 532–534.

Problem-Solving Strategy:
Make an Organized List

Ask Yourself

Understand What facts do I know?

Plan Did I make an organized list?

Solve How can I show all of the possibilities?
Do I need to cross out duplicates?

Look Back Did I solve the problem?

Make an organized list to solve each problem.

1. Leon, Bess, Karen, and Donna are finalists
in a spelling bee. The top two finalists
win trophies (without distinguishing first
and second place). How many different
ways can the trophies be awarded?

_____

2. The elective classes offered at Wilson
Middle school are cooking, wood shop,
art, drafting, and band. Each student
selects 3 of these classes. How many
different groups of 3 electives are
possible?

_____

3. Jack, Trisha, Sam, Hoon, Chloe, and
Sean are running for two class offices.
How many different pairs can win the
election?

_____

Use with text pages 536–538.

Experimental Probability

To find the **experimental probability** of an event, compare the number of favorable outcomes with the total number of completed trials.

For Problems 1–2, select 4 blue cubes, 1 yellow cube, and 5 red cubes—a total of 10 cubes. Place them in a bag. Then use the recording sheet to complete each probability experiment.

1. Find the experimental probability of selecting a blue cube. Then pick a cube, tally the result, and return the cube to the bag. Pick 20 times.

EXPERIMENT RESULTS					
Event	Theoretical Probability	Prediction ? times in ? trials	Tally of Favorable Outcomes	Number of Favorable Outcomes	Experimental Probability
Blue					

2. Find the experimental probability of selecting a yellow cube. Then pick a cube, tally the result, and return the cube to the bag. Pick 20 times.

EXPERIMENT RESULTS					
Event	Theoretical Probability	Prediction ? times in ? trials	Tally of Favorable Outcomes	Number of Favorable Outcomes	Experimental Probability
Yellow					

Problem Solving

Show Your Work

3. How are theoretical probability and experimental probability alike? How do they differ?

_____

Use with text pages 540–542.

Compound Events

Ways to Find the Probability of a Compound Event

Suppose you toss a penny and roll a number cube labeled 1–6. What is the probability of the coin landing on tails, and the cube landing on an even number?

Use a tree diagram.

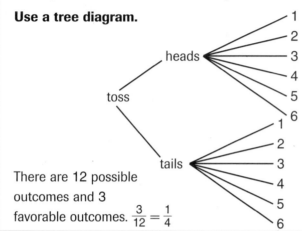

There are 12 possible outcomes and 3 favorable outcomes. $\frac{3}{12} = \frac{1}{4}$

Use an organized list.

heads, 1	tails, 1
heads, 2	tails, 2
heads, 3	tails, 3
heads, 4	tails, 4
heads, 5	tails, 5
heads, 6	tails, 6

There are 12 possible outcomes and 3 favorable outcomes. $\frac{3}{12} = \frac{1}{4}$

Suppose you spin each spinner once. Find the probability of each compound event.

1. white and 1

_____

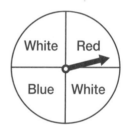

2. red and an even number

_____

3. blue and a number less than 2

_____

4. red or white and an odd number

_____

5. red and a number greater than 5

_____

6. white and 3 or 4

_____

7. blue or white and a number greater than 1

_____

Problem Solving

8. Use the spinners shown above to describe a compound event with a probability of 1.

_____

Show Your Work

Use with text pages 544–545.

Problem-Solving Application:
Make Predictions

Ask Yourself	
Understand	What does the question ask me to find?
Plan	Did I use the formula for probability?
Solve	Did I use the correct information?
	Did I find the probability of the event?
	Did I use the probability to make a prediction?
Look Back	Does my answer make sense?

Use the table to solve Problems 1–2.

Show Your Work

Number of People on the Bus		
	Bus A	Bus B
Girls	22	8
Boys	15	23

1. What is the probability of selecting a girl at random from Bus A? Bus B?

_____

2. What is the probability of selecting a boy at random from either bus?

_____

3. Rhoda surveyed 30 classmates and found that 18 own a pet. Based on her data, how many students in a group of 500 would likely own a pet?

_____

Use with text pages 546–548.

Name _____ Date _____

Model Equations

> An **equation** is a mathematical sentence showing that two mathematical expressions are equal. $x + 4 = 14$ is an example of an equation.

1. In $x + 5 = 11$, what does x represent?

_____

2. Add 4 to both sides of $x + 5 = 11$. What value does x represent?

_____

3. Subtract 2 from both sides of $x + 5 = 11$. What value does x represent?

_____

4. In $3x = 15$, what does x represent?

_____

5. Multiply both sides of $3x = 15$ by 2. What value does x represent?

_____

6. Divide both sides of $3x = 15$ by 3. What value does x represent?

_____

Problem Solving

7. Describe two ways of changing the equation $x + 4 = 8$ without changing the value of x.

_____

Show Your Work

Use with text pages 566–567.

Write and Solve Equations

Use Inverse Operations to Solve Equations			
Addition and Subtraction		Multiplication and Division	
$x + 8 = 12$	$x - 9 = 17$	$7x = 42$	$x \div 2 = 12$
$x + 8 - 8 = 12 - 8$	$x - 9 + 9 = 17 + 9$	$7x \div 7 = 42 \div 7$	$(x \div 2) \times 2 = 12 \times 2$
$x + 0 = 4$	$x - 0 = 26$	$1 \times x = 6$	$x \div 1 = 24$
$x = 4$	$x = 26$	$x = 6$	$x = 24$

Solve using inverse operations.

1. $t \div 7 = 10$ **2.** $52 = 4k$ **3.** $d \div 4 = 5$ **4.** $19 + b = 38$

_____   _____   _____   _____

5. $r - 45 = 17$ **6.** $55s = 165$ **7.** $81 \div p = 9$ **8.** $12h = 132$

_____   _____   _____   _____

9. $u \div 8 = 16$ **10.** $217 + c = 335$ **11.** $19q = 76$ **12.** $b - 89 = 113$

_____   _____   _____   _____

13. $155 + s = 249$ **14.** $r - 54 = 29$ **15.** $341 + m = 500$ **16.** $a - 99 = 176$

_____   _____   _____   _____

Problem Solving

17. What value for a makes this equation true? $5a = a$

_____

Show Your Work

Use with text pages 568–570.

Problem-Solving Strategy: Write an Equation

Ask Yourself	
Understand	What facts do I know?
Plan	Did I write an equation?
Solve	Did I use a variable to represent what I need to know?
	Did I use the correct operation to solve the equation?
Look Back	Does my answer make sense?

Write an equation to solve each problem.

Show Your Work

1. Lydia has a weekly salary of $645. This is $67 more than Dora's weekly salary. What is Dora's weekly salary?

   _____

2. Chung earned $24,720 last year. If he earned the same amount each month, what was Chung's monthly salary?

   _____

3. Leticia baby-sits for $4.50 an hour. She is saving her money for a bus ticket to a kids' Science Camp. She needs $22.50 more to pay for the ticket. How many more hours does she need to baby-sit before she has enough money?

   _____

4. Nikko is helping his dad plant a bed of tulips in front of their house. Six large tulip bulbs come in a bag for $7.50. They paid $150 for tulips. How many bags did they buy?

   _____

Use with text pages 572–574.

Variable and Functions

Use a function table to find values for the function $y = 5 + x$.

- Replace x in the fuction rule with values for x from the first column of the function table. Then use the rule to solve for y.

- Remember: In a function table, there is **exactly one entry** in the second column (y) for every entry in the first column (x)z

- For the function rule $y = 5 + x$:
  If $x = 1$, then $y = 5 + 1 = 6$.
  If $x = 2$, then $y = 5 + 2 = 7$.
  If $x = 3$, then $y = 5 + 3 = 8$.
  If $x = 4$, then $y = 5 + 4 = 9$.

Function Table

enter
$x \longrightarrow$
values

x	y
1	6
2	7
3	8
4	9

solve
for
y
values

Copy and complete each function table.

1. $y = 14 - x$

x	y
0	____
1	____
2	____
3	____

2. $y = 7x$

x	y
0	____
1	____
2	____
3	____

3. $y = 36 \div x$

x	y
1	____
2	____
3	____
4	____

Problem Solving

Show Your Work

4. There are 8 servings in one bag of popcorn. Make a function table to show how many servings are in 2, 3, 4, and 5 bags of popcorn.

_____

Use with text pages 576–577.

Patterns and Functions

Different Ways to Represent a Function		
Use a function table.		**Use an equation.**

Classes	Total Students
1	24
2	48
3	72
4	96

Let x = number of classes

Let y = total students

$$y = 24x$$

Copy and complete each function table.

1. $y = 20x + 2$

x	y
0	___
1	___
2	___
3	___

2. $y = 35 - 2x$

x	y
0	___
___	29
___	25
7	___

3. $y = 6x + 13$

x	y
0	___
2	___
___	37
___	49

Use the function table. Find the value of y for the given value of x.

4. If $x = 7$, $y =$ ___

x	y
0	1
1	5
2	9
3	13

5. If $x = 8$, $y =$ ___

x	y
0	8
2	12
4	16
6	20

6. If $x = 5$, $y =$ ___

x	y
0	25
1	22
2	19
3	16

Problem Solving

Show Your Work

7. Beth is 4 years older than Jill. Write and solve an equation to find Jill's age if Beth is 22 years old.

_____

Use with text pages 578–581.

Name _____ Date _____

Integers and Absolute Value

Finding Absolute Value

A number's distance from zero is called its **absolute value.** What is the absolute value of ⁻6?

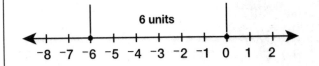

The absolute value of ⁻6 is 6.

6 units

Write the opposite of each integer.

1. ⁻12   **2.** ⁻5   **3.** ⁺18   **4.** ⁺29

_____   _____   _____   _____

5. ⁺73   **6.** ⁻92   **7.** ⁻317   **8.** ⁺47

_____   _____   _____   _____

9. ⁻55   **10.** ⁺118   **11.** ⁺60   **12.** ⁻212

_____   _____   _____   _____

Write the absolute value of each integer.

13. 0   **14.** ⁻16   **15.** ⁺77   **16.** ⁻4

_____   _____   _____   _____

17. ⁺9   **18.** ⁻15   **19.** ⁺22   **20.** ⁻11

_____   _____   _____   _____

21. ⁺10   **22.** ⁻24   **23.** ⁻13   **24.** ⁺34

_____   _____   _____   _____

Problem Solving

Show Your Work

25. Name a pair of integers with the same absolute value.

_____

               Use with text pages 586–587.

Name _____ Date _____

Compare and Order Integers

Comparing Integers

Order 1, ⁻2 and ⁻3 from least to greatest.

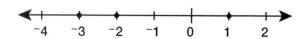

The integer farthest to the left is the least, and the integer farthest to the right is the greatest.

⁻3 < ⁻2 < ⁺1

Compare. Draw a number line from ⁻8 to ⁺8 and label each integer. Write >, <, or = for each ◯.

1. ⁺3 ◯ 0

2. ⁻1 ◯ ⁻4

3. ⁻5 ◯ ⁻1

4. ⁻2 ◯ 0

5. ⁺1 ◯ ⁺4

6. ⁻5 ◯ ⁻2

7. ⁻1 ◯ ⁻7

8. ⁺4 ◯ ⁻3

9. ⁻5 ◯ ⁻7

10. ⁻1 ◯ ⁺1

11. ⁺5 ◯ 0

12. ⁻4 ◯ ⁻6

13. 0 ◯ ⁻7

14. ⁻3 ◯ ⁺2

15. ⁺4 ◯ ⁻4

16. ⁻5 ◯ ⁻4

Write the integers in order from least to greatest. Draw a number line if you wish.

17. ⁻4, ⁻7, ⁻3, 0

18. ⁺3, ⁻5, ⁺2, ⁻1

_____

_____

19. ⁻12, ⁺8, ⁻9, ⁺10

20. ⁺1, ⁻3, ⁻2, ⁺2

_____

_____

Problem Solving

Show Your Work

21. At 6 A.M. the temperature in Oakville was between ⁻1°F and ⁻5°F. Name three possible temperatures in Oakville at 6 A.M.

_____

Use with text pages 588–590.

Model Addition of Integers

Find $^-4 + {}^+5$.

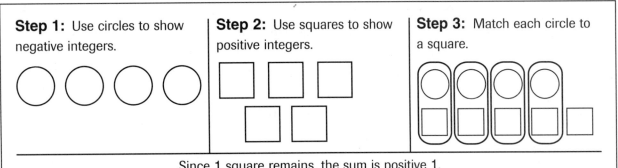

Step 1: Use circles to show negative integers.

Step 2: Use squares to show positive integers.

Step 3: Match each circle to a square.

Since 1 square remains, the sum is positive 1.

$$^-4 + {}^+5 = {}^+1$$

Write the addition expression shown by the circles and squares and then find the sum.

1. ☐ ☐ ☐ ◯

_____

2. ◯ ◯ ◯ ◯ ◯ ☐ ☐

_____

Use models to find each sum.

3. $^+8 + {}^-6$ 4. $^-7 + {}^-5$ 5. $^-7 + {}^+2$ 6. $^-9 + {}^+8$

_____   _____   _____   _____

7. $^+6 + {}^-10$ 8. $^-11 + {}^+6$ 9. $^-3 + {}^-2$ 10. $^+10 + {}^-3$

_____   _____   _____   _____

Use models to find each sum. Then compare. Write >, <, or =.

11. $^-7 + {}^+2$ ◯ $^+1 + {}^-6$ 12. $^+8 + {}^-7$ ◯ $0 + {}^-5$ 13. $^-2 + {}^-9$ ◯ $^+15 + {}^-4$

Problem Solving

Show Your Work

14. At noon the temperature was 54°F. At sunset the temperature was 50°F. Write an integer to represent the change in temperature.

_____

Use with text pages 592–594.

Name _____ Date _____

Model Subtraction of Integers

Find $^-3 - {}^+1$.

Step 1: Use circles to show negative integers. Use squares to show positive integers.

Step 2: You need to subtract $^+1$ but there are no squares to take away. Add a circle and a square to show 0.

Step 3: Take away a square to subtract $^+1$. What is left?

Since 4 circles remain, the difference is negative 4.

$$^-3 - {}^+1 = {}^-4$$

Write a subtraction expression for each. Then find the difference.

1.

Take away 2 squares.

_____

2.

Take away 7 circles.

_____

Use models to find each difference.

3. $^+1 - {}^-5$ 4. $^-2 - {}^+3$ 5. $^-6 - {}^-1$ 6. $^+2 - {}^-2$

_____   _____   _____   _____

7. $^+9 - {}^-11$ 8. $^-7 - {}^-5$ 9. $^+8 - {}^-5$ 10. $^+8 - {}^-1$

_____   _____   _____   _____

11. $^+12 - {}^+9$ 12. $^-11 - {}^-6$ 13. $^+7 - {}^-3$ 14. $^-5 - {}^+10$

_____   _____   _____   _____

Problem Solving

Show Your Work

15. Amy deposited $25 into her savings account. Later that month she withdrew $17. What integer shows the net change in the amount of money in her account?

_____

Use with text pages 596–597.

Add and Subtract Integers

Rules for Adding and Subtracting Integers

- You can turn any subtraction expression into addition by adding the opposite
- The sum of two positive integers is positive.
- The sum of two negative integers is negative.
- The sum of a positive integer and a negative integer will have the same sign as the integer with the greater absolute value.

Decide whether the answer will be positive or negative. Then use the number line to add or subtract.

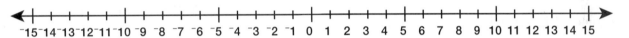

⁻15 ⁻14 ⁻13 ⁻12 ⁻11 ⁻10 ⁻9 ⁻8 ⁻7 ⁻6 ⁻5 ⁻4 ⁻3 ⁻2 ⁻1 0 1 2 3 4 5 6 7 8 9 10 11 12 13 14 15

1. $0 + {}^{+}6$ **2.** ${}^{-}3 - {}^{-}11$ **3.** ${}^{-}9 + {}^{+}1$ **4.** ${}^{+}6 - {}^{-}4$

_____   _____   _____   _____

5. ${}^{-}11 - {}^{+}4$ **6.** ${}^{-}12 + {}^{+}8$ **7.** ${}^{+}3 - {}^{-}6$ **8.** ${}^{+}4 + {}^{-}7$

_____   _____   _____   _____

9. ${}^{+}6 + {}^{-}9$ **10.** ${}^{-}12 - {}^{-}5$ **11.** ${}^{-}5 + 0$ **12.** ${}^{+}8 - {}^{-}2$

_____   _____   _____   _____

Problem Solving

Show Your Work

13. Stacey got on an elevator on the ground floor. She rode up 8 floors, then down 5 floors and got off. On what floor did Stacey get off the elevator?

_____

Use with text pages 598–600.

Problem-Solving Application:
Use Integers

Solve.

Show Your Work

1. A diver descended 7 meters below the water's surface. The diver then swam down another 4 meters. What integer shows the diver's position in relation to the water's surface?

   _____

2. A bus left the station with 30 riders. At the first stop, 7 riders left the bus and 3 got on. At the second stop, 8 riders left the bus and 2 got on. What integer shows the change in the number of riders on the bus after the second stop?

   _____

3. Peg stood at 0 on a starting line. She then moved 5 steps backward, 2 steps forward, and 3 steps backward. What integer shows her position in relation to 0 on the starting line?

   _____

Use with text pages 602–604.

Integers and the Coordinate Plane

- A coordinate plane is formed by two perpendicular lines called axes that lie in the plane.
- The horizontal axis is called the *x*-axis, and the vertical axis is called the *y*-axis.
- The axes divide the grid into 4 quadrants, numbered I, II, III, and IV.
- Every point on a coordinate plane is named by an ordered pair, (*x, y*).
- The point named by the ordered pair (0, 0) is the origin.

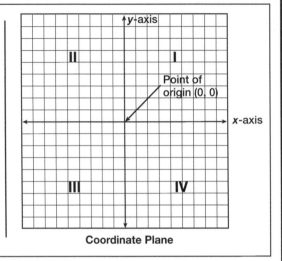

Coordinate Plane

Use the graph for Problems 1–12. Write the ordered pair for each point.

1. *I* _____

2. *A* _____

3. *C* _____

4. *B* _____

5. *P* _____

6. *H* _____

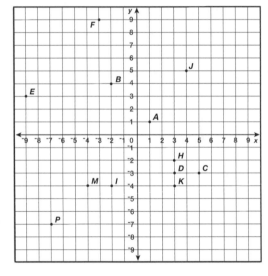

Write the letter name for each point.

7. ($^-$9, $^+$3) _____

8. ($^+$4, $^+$5) _____

9. ($^+$3, $^-$4) _____

10. ($^-$4, $^-$4) _____

11. ($^-$3, $^+$9) _____

12. (3, $^-$3) _____

Problem Solving

Show Your Work

13. If you plotted the points ($^-$3, $^-$3), ($^-$3, $^+$3), ($^+$3, $^+$3), and ($^+$3, $^-$3) and connected the points in that order, what shape would form?

_____

Use with text pages 610–612.

Integers and Functions

$y = 3x - 4$

Step 1: Make a function table.

Step 2: Choose values for x.
Write them in the table.

Step 3: Substitute each value of x into the function to find the value of y.

If $x = 1$, then $y = 3(1) - 4 = {}^-1$
If $x = 2$, then $y = 3(2) - 4 = 2$
If $x = 3$, then $y = 3(3) - 4 = 5$
If $x = 4$, then $y = 3(4) - 4 = 8$

$y = 3x - 4$

x	y
1	⁻1
2	2
3	5
4	8

Complete the function table.

1. $y = x + 4$

x	y
⁻3	
⁻2	
⁻1	
0	

2. $y = x - 3$

x	y
⁻2	
0	
2	
5	

3. $y = 6 - x$

x	y
⁻2	
⁻1	
0	
3	

4. $y = 4x$

x	y
0	
1	
2	
3	

5. $y = x - 6$

x	y
⁻3	
0	
3	
6	

6. $y = 7x$

x	y
0	
1	
2	
3	

Problem Solving

Show Your Work

7. The first two sets of pairs of values in a function table are $({}^-3, {}^-2)$ and $({}^-2, {}^-1)$. What is the function?

_____

Use with text pages 614–615.

Use Functions and Graphs

How to Graph an Equation		
Step 1: Make a function table to find the ordered pairs.	**Step 2:** Graph each ordered pair.	**Step 3:** Extend the line.

Find the values of y to complete each function table. Then graph each equation as a straight line on grid paper.

1. $y = 4x - 2$

x	y
0	
1	
2	
3	

2. $y = 3x + 2$

x	y
0	
1	
2	
3	

Find three ordered pairs for each function. Then use them to graph the function.

3. $y = 8x$

4. $y = 2x + 5$

5. $y = 3x - 4$

6. $y = x + 3$

_____   _____   _____   _____

_____   _____   _____   _____

_____   _____   _____   _____

Problem Solving

Show Your Work

7. Graph the lines $y = 1x$ and $y = -1x$ on the same coordinate plane. How are they the same and how are they different?

_____

_____

_____

_____

Use with text pages 616–618.

Name _____ Date _____

Problem-Solving Application:
Use a Graph

Ask Yourself	
Understand	What do I need to find?
Plan	Did I record the correct information?
Solve	What patterns do I see?
Look Back	Is my answer reasonable?

Solve. Use the table for Problems 1–2.

Show Your Work

Campers	4	8	12	16
Counselors	1	2	3	4

1. As the number of campers at the Summers-'R-Best Camp grew, the staff needed to hire more camp counselors. Write an equation to show the relationship between the number of counselors (c) and the number of campers (p).

   _____

   _____

2. Solve the equation to find the number of counselors needed when 600 campers attend the program.

   _____

   _____

Solve. Use the graph for Problems 3–4.

3. Write an equation for the data shown in the graph using s for students and c for candy sold.

   _____

   _____

4. Use the equation to find how much candy 100 students would sell.

   _____

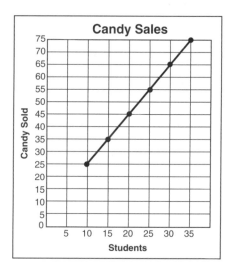

152

Use with text pages 620–621.

Name _____ Date _____

Transformations in the Coordinate Plane

- A **transformation** is a change in the position of a figure on a graph.
- A **reflection** is a flip of a figure that results in a mirror image.
- A **rotation** is a turn around a given point. One complete turn is 360°.
- A figure has **rotational symmetry** if it looks exactly the same after being rotated less than 360° around a center point.

Use the diagram. Name the coordinates of triangle ABC after the transformations.

1. Reflect over the *y*-axis.

_____

2. Translate right 1, then down 2

_____

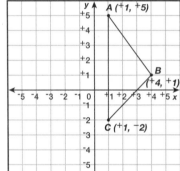

3. Rotate $\frac{1}{4}$ a turn around (0, 0)

_____

4. Translate left 3, then up 1

_____

Write *line*, *rotational*, or *both* to describe the symmetry of the figure.

5.

_____

6.

_____

Problem Solving _____

Show Your Work

7. If a point is located at $(-1, -1)$ and it shifts up 1 and to the right 1, where is it now located?

_____

153   **Use with text pages 622–624.**